A DOG FOR ALL SEASONS

A DOG FOR ALL SEASONS

A Memoir

Patti Sherlock

THOMAS DUNNE BOOKS
ST. MARTIN'S PRESS
NEW YORK

THOMAS DUNNE BOOKS.
An imprint of St. Martin's Press.

A DOG FOR ALL SEASONS. Copyright © 2010 by Patti Sherlock. All rights reserved. Printed in the United States of America. For information, address St. Martin's Press, 175 Fifth Avenue, New York, N.Y. 10010.

Design by Susan Walsh

Library of Congress Cataloging-in-Publication Data

Sherlock, Patti.
    A dog for all seasons / Patti Sherlock.—1st ed.
        p. cm.
    ISBN 978-0-312-57792-6 (alk. paper)
    1. Border collie—Idaho—Biography.   2. Sheep—Idaho.
3. Sherlock, Patti. I. Title.
    SF429.B64S54 2010
    636.737'40929—dc22   2009040296

First Edition: April 2010

10 9 8 7 6 5 4 3 2 1

To my remarkable sister,
the late Bobbette Clark,
who embraced all changing seasons
with gratitude

AUTHOR'S NOTE

The reader may note stories in the book don't always correspond to the seasonal title they fall under. Just as winter sometimes has sparkling, sunshiny days and spring has dark and gloomy ones, events sometimes fall into a cycle of development rather than a particular month. I hope the reader won't mind my figurative use of the section titles.

PROLOGUE

My headlamp cut a cylinder of light through the blowing snow. I trudged toward the barn, trying to follow indistinct tracks I'd made only an hour before.

Duncan, my Border collie pup, hopped over three-foot drifts. He stopped to bite at a chunk of snow. Then he dashed ahead, turned and wagged, and raced on. Somehow, he didn't notice it was 2 A.M. and 12 degrees with a raging wind.

A ski mask covered my face, and I'd zipped my coveralls to my chin. Even so, stinging flakes hit exposed places on my neck and gathered on my eyelashes.

My husband, George, and I took turns covering the barn at night during lambing. He worked a day job and couldn't be up every night; I had a busy daytime schedule with three young children. Every other night one of us got a full night's sleep, unless wakened by the other to help.

Many nights I liked the dark, silent walk to the barn. Stars were a million side-by-side pinholes. I liked when I slid open the barn door and rich animal scent filled my nose. The barn would be many degrees warmer than outside from straw bales banked against the walls, and from the ewes themselves, contentedly chewing cud and waiting for their lambs to arrive.

But on a January night like this, cold and wind slapped me awake and even if I found no new lambs, I'd have a hard time getting back to sleep.

Duncan waited for me beside the barn door, wriggling with excitement.

"If there's a first-time mother, you'll have to go outside," I warned him.

Veteran ewes tolerated Duncan. They would stomp a front foot to warn him if he came too close to a lambing jug, a temporary pen we constructed from wooden pallets, but mostly they stayed intent on mothering their newborns. But a first-time mother might feel so jittery about a dog being around that she couldn't settle down and concentrate on her lambs.

When I stepped inside the barn I knew there'd be no returning to bed. I heard a ewe going "Maa-aa-aa" in a low voice. Ewes made this deep chuckle only after dropping a lamb.

I shone my headlamp in a circle. The light found Buttercup, one of my favorite ewes, standing beside a wet lamb. Buttercup was lick, lick, licking the lamb like she meant to take off its hide. The lamb held its head up and blatted. It was only minutes old, still wet, and strong. It was good to find lambs when they were only a few minutes old. I'd have the lamb under a heat lamp in a few minutes, and it would avoid the stress of getting cold.

Normally, Buttercup was an easygoing creature who might have paid the dog no heed, but the light showed a water bag hanging from her rear end; she had another lamb on the way.

"You better stay back," I told Duncan, who politely sat down on a grain sack.

By the time I'd scattered fresh straw in a lambing jug, Buttercup's second lamb was on the ground. She took to licking it as she had the first. Now she had to clean up the new lamb and also keep working on the first. Another water bag appeared; no surprise, Buttercup usually had triplets.

I picked up the first lamb, held it out in front of me, and walked backward to the jug. Buttercup blatted and followed me into the enclosure. I tied the jug shut and settled the lambs under a heat lamp. Then I sat down in the stall beside Buttercup, a towel in my hand. "Looks like you need help." I picked up one of the lambs and started rubbing it hard to get its circulation going.

Duncan eased closer.

"You can come a little ways," I said.

He inched forward, shyly.

"That's far enough," I said when he got ten feet away.

Duncan laid down and put his head on his paws. He savvied he had to maintain a polite distance now, yet, the next day he would chase ewes relentlessly to help me sort them.

Buttercup dropped her third lamb. She licked the gooey sack off its head so it could breathe. I got busy dipping lambs' navels in iodine; then I helped each of them find their way to Buttercup's engorged milk bag.

Getting up on a cold night was an aggravation, but participating in an uncomplicated birth was a joy that went marrow deep. I was present for something primal—life asserting itself. This was the joyful aspect of the life-death parade, and I got to be a spectator.

I went outside to draw a bucket of water for Buttercup, then came back and walked among the other ewes. Most of them didn't get up. I looked to see if any looked restless, an indication they might lamb soon, but all looked content.

"Come on, Duncan." I started for the house, then remembered I ought to check behind the barn to see if any of the ewes had wandered outside through the barn's small back door.

I found three ewes lying down outside. All had blue ear tags, which meant they were yearlings. I didn't recognize them—they either were ones I didn't know or it was hard to see in blowing snow. I shone my headlamp on each. When I got to the third, I stopped. I noticed blood around her tail. Sometime between this barn check and the one three hours before, she had lambed.

"What are you doing out here!" I scolded. Most of our ewes, even young ones, went into the barn to lamb. Ones who failed to do this George and I labeled dumb and culled from our breeding program.

This yearling lay only a few feet from the barn door, which baffled me. Why hadn't she gone a few more feet to get out of the wind?

"Where is your lamb?" I demanded. It could be anywhere in the

large pen, probably dead. With Duncan trotting beside me, I searched
the pen, shining my light in what I hoped was a systematic grid. I
couldn't find the lamb. By now, it might be covered by blowing snow.

I went back to the yearling, who still was lying down, legs tucked
under her. The other two young ewes had gotten up and gone into
the barn.

"Why aren't *you* looking for your lamb?" I leaned over then and
saw it was Lark, a beautiful young ewe from one of our best families. Usually, ewes carrying this heredity showed strong mothering
skills.

Maybe her lamb had been born dead and she'd given up on it and
deserted it. Still, why had she lambed outside? I would have expected
better.

I tapped her rear end with my foot. "Get up, I need to check if
you have more coming."

She refused to move.

"Well, you are nothing like your mother."

I grabbed her around the neck and pulled her to her feet. And
then I saw the reason for her stubbornness. Lying against the fence,
eyes closed, was a newborn lamb. My heart sunk.

Duncan touched his nose to the lamb's head. He perked his ears
and wagged at me.

"Don't get too excited. That lamb looks half dead."

The lamb was immaculate; Lark had polished him to a gleaming
white. I started to concoct a different theory. Lark probably had lambed
indoors after all, cleaned up the lamb, and then it had wandered outside. She had followed. When the lamb got wedged in a hollow beside the fence and couldn't get out, she'd laid down on him to keep
him warm.

I stroked Lark's ear. "I'll try to save him."

The lamb was frozen to the snow. Parts of him had been kept
warm by his mother, but his rear legs were stuck to icy ground. His
neck was limp and he made no response to my tugging on him. I
went back in the barn for a hammer. Using the claw end for prying,

I managed to free the lamb's legs from the snow. Lark hung over me, blatting nonstop to the lamb.

I carried the lamb to the house, calling over my shoulder to his mother, "I'll be back." I could feel a faint heartbeat in his skinny chest.

I debated whether to waken George, but reviving a cold lamb was a one-person job. I filled the bathroom sink with body temperature water; the warming needed to be gradual to avoid shocking the lamb's heart. I lowered the lamb into the sink, immersing everything but his head, which I kept lifted. The lamb gave a small, pitiful bleat.

Cylinders of ice that encased the lamb's legs began to crack. After only a minute, the water in the basin turned icy. I removed the lamb, wrapped him in a towel, refilled the basin with warm water, and repeated the process. Duncan sat on one of my cold feet.

When the lamb no longer felt alarmingly cold to the touch, I carried him back to the kitchen. His eyes stayed shut, his neck hung limp over my arm. I took cubes of colostrum, a ewe's first milk, from the ice cube tray in the freezer and placed them in a pan to heat at a low temperature. Overheating colostrum could kill the elements that helped to build immunities.

I got out the plastic tube and syringe. Hypothermia made lambs lose their sucking reflex, so this lamb would refuse to drink from a bottle. I disliked tubing a lamb, always worrying that in my tiredness I might send fluid down the wrong pipe and into the lamb's lungs. But I'd also seen how much difference high-energy colostrum could make to a dying lamb.

I sat on the floor and began to ease the tube down the lamb's throat. Duncan sat beside me watching, head tilted. Every few seconds I put the tube to my ear, listening for air to make sure I hadn't gone into the lamb's lung.

When the tube was in the lamb's belly, I attached a syringe full of warm colostrum and pumped the end. The colostrum emptied into the lamb's belly. I placed him in a cardboard box lined with newspaper.

I patted Duncan. "That's all I can do for a while. I need to go check Buttercup's lambs. Would you babysit?"

At the kitchen door, Duncan tried to slip out with me. "No, go back and stay with the lamb."

Disappointed, he dropped his head but walked back to the box.

I found the newborn triplets sleeping peacefully beside their mother. Buttercup gazed at me with tranquil yellow eyes and a look of pride.

I did a quick check of other new lambs and their mothers, then shone my light on the drop herd, ewes that would lamb soon. Lark followed at my heels, blatting piteously.

"Maybe in the morning you'll have him back," I told her.

I trudged back to the house. Duncan met me at the door with a worried face.

"What's wrong?"

He ran ahead of me to the box, which was empty. The lamb I'd almost written off for dead had upended the box and now was loose in the house. A puddle of urine glistened under the kitchen's fluorescent light.

I found the lamb in the living room, his hooves clicking on the wooden floor like tap shoes. He blatted so loudly I wondered that my family hadn't wakened. Sticky, black meconium oozed from his rear end. I smiled. His plumbing worked.

Duncan ran to me, then back to the lamb. He knew something was amiss for a lamb to be running loose. I grabbed the lamb and deposited him into the box. I tore up another box and built up the sides of the first box with cardboard strips and duct tape. It was gratifying to be reinforcing confinement for a lamb I'd chipped from the ice an hour before. That's how it was, though, with lambs and colostrum. Baby lambs could show great desire to live, and colostrum acted like a magic potion. I told Duncan goodnight and went to bed.

In the morning I woke before it was light. Even before I became totally awake, I sensed that something was wrong. After I roused more, I knew what it was. The house was totally silent. By now, the lamb should be hungry again.

I eased out of bed. Duncan met me when I opened the bedroom door and preceded me to the kitchen.

The lamb lay sprawled in the box, eyes shut. Even before I picked him up, I heard him rasping. The sound of pneumonia. Had signs of pneumonia been there the night before and I hadn't noticed? Lambs could get pneumonia from drafts and germs, but this probably was mechanical pneumonia, from swallowing amniotic fluid during the birthing process or from being tubed incorrectly. At the time, I'd thought the tubing had gone well, but those hours in the night were a blur now.

Pneumonia, the mechanical kind, was fatal. I'd heard of a few cases where someone had pulled a lamb through using heroic methods, but in those instances, the person had only a couple of lambs to care for. More lambs were on their way at our house, and caring for those already on the ground took a great deal of time.

George got up, then the boys, Matt and Shane, then Mary. Newborns were irresistibly cuddly, but no one picked up this lamb. It looked frail, and its breathing sounded like sticks clicking together.

"Will he be okay?" Mary, who was five, asked. I traded a look with George.

"He's very sick," I answered.

George said he'd drive Mary to kindergarten so I could get busy on the barn chores. The boys went off to catch the school bus and the house got quiet again.

I changed the wet newspaper in the box. I wouldn't be back in the house for hours and regretted that the lamb might die alone in a silent, empty house. I couldn't put him back with his mother; it would only confuse her, and besides, she might paw at him, urging him to get up.

I fed hay to the mothers in jugs, then to the drop herd, then to ewes in the pasture. I noticed that winter sun beaming overhead had melted the snow off my car. When I touched the hood, it felt warm. I went to the house and fetched the lamb and placed him on the warm metal. Now he had a light, sunny place to die.

He lay motionless, eyes closed, rattling like a gourd.

I went to the porch and sat on the top step. The cement felt cold and hard against my butt, even though I was wearing insulated coveralls.

Duncan sat a step below me. He gazed into space, ears alert, like he was expecting someone. Or maybe he wasn't watching for anything, maybe he was listening.

"I wonder how much of this I can take." I sighed.

Duncan turned and pointed his nose at my face. He gazed into my eyes in a wise, Border collie way. I was a grown-up person and he was a pup, but I wished he could weigh in on the matter. If dogs had psychic powers, maybe Duncan could give me a number—how many deaths I'd need to witness in this helpless fashion.

Duncan moved up a stair to join me. He sat down close and leaned his body against my chest. His face remained upturned, his eyes intense.

I was falling into the dog lovers' pitfall, trying to impose human thoughts on a canine. Maybe he only looked understanding and had no idea what I was feeling. Maybe if he did know my distress he had no sympathy for it, because dogs don't fret the future. Maybe Duncan had concerns of his own, like thoughts of delicious bones or pancakes.

But I didn't believe that. He snuggled so close, I thought at the very least he meant to convey warmth on this chilly morning.

His eyes communicated something more. An answer? I read in them, *You can take quite a bit.*

I told him, "I'm putting words in your mouth. And I don't like what you're saying."

Duncan repositioned himself. There was no space between us as it was, but he got closer, melting into my coveralls.

I understood then what he was trying to communicate.

However much there is, I'm here.

Spring

ONE

I stood in an open field on the Charlie Kimball ranch in Central Idaho.
In distant corrals, I could see sheep milling, looking like white foam
washing up on the hillside. A breeze coming off the blue peaks behind the ranch caused me to zip up my jacket. It was August, but already early morning had a fall-like feel.

George and I had left our home in Idaho Falls before sunup with
a sleepyheaded Mary; Matt and Shane had preferred to stay in bed on
a Saturday. We'd come to buy a new ram for our growing flock of
ewes. For me, the day would be fateful.

We were raising a new sheep breed, the Polypay. At national sales
we'd attended, sheep consigned by fellow Idahoan Charlie Kimball
had impressed us. Kimball ran a range sheep operation, grazing 3,000
head on government land near Sun Valley, the famous Idaho resort and
celebrity hangout.

We followed Charlie to his corrals. Four-year-old Mary wrested
her hand from mine and ran off.

"Don't scare the sheep," I called.

"Let her run," Charlie said. Tall, white-haired, taller still in straw
cowboy hat and boots, he glided over the ground with huge strides.
George and I had to stretch our steps to keep up.

When we got to the pens, I said, "Wow!" The rams looked
beautiful—muscular and masculine with handsome faces and tight
fleeces.

I got to be the one who selected our rams because of a lucky first
experience a few years before. I'd purchased our first ram by myself,
relying on blind luck and advice from a passerby. The ram I took home

turned out to be an exceptional producer whose daughters gave birth to numerous multiples. George would say how much we could spend for a ram; I would employ intuition and consider aesthetics when deciding on one.

"Get in there," George said to me, "and see what you like." He climbed over the fence and started moving the rams toward me.

We wanted our rams to have straight legs with good bone and a wide stance, characteristics they would pass to their daughters, the ewes that would build our flock. The best of our ram lambs would be sold for breeding, but most males would be castrated to become meat wethers, so we wanted good meat characteristics, too. I'd learned to tell quality of loin and legs by feeling the sheep with my hands, which is what I set about doing.

Suitability for breeding had to be considered, too, and examining testicles for circumference and attachment was part of ram selection. (In future years, I would let it drop in polite company that I was something of a testicle expert, having handled hundreds of sets.)

For the next hour, George and Charlie caught candidates and held them while I checked loins, legs, testicles, and wool. Mary hung on the fence, pointing. "I like that one, Mommy. Check him."

We narrowed the field to two beautiful yearlings. We would breed the daughters of one to the other and not have to go ram shopping again for a couple of years.

"Could we look at their papers?" George asked.

Charlie pushed back his hat. "I misunderstood. I thought you were looking for commercial rams. I've been too busy to keep up the paperwork for purebred registry."

I should have remembered to check that on the phone.

"You going to stay strictly purebred?" he asked.

We nodded. As purebred breeders we could offer careful records on ancestry, productivity, and weight gain so buyers could improve the quality of their sheep. But it was disappointing not to take home a beautiful Kimball ram.

"Come up to the house for coffee," Charlie said. "And you'll want to see the pups."

I stopped walking and scowled at the ground. Pups were a tender subject with me.

By now, the August sun had warmed things and cobalt sky stretched from one horizon to the other. Charlie glided ahead of us, talking about signs of early winter. On his summer range, the aspens were turning yellow and his horses already had shaggy hair.

Roma, Charlie's wife, waved from the porch, where she sat snapping beans into a bowl. A black-and-white Border collie pup gnawed on her shoe. Three other pups and the bitch came running out from under a farm wagon.

One pup charged up to me. I picked it up. It squirmed, licked, and tested razor teeth on my chin. "I want to hold him," Mary said, so I put the wriggler in her arms. He raked her chin with his claws and she dropped him. The pup scrambled to his feet and began to paw at her legs. Mary ran away and climbed onto the wagon tongue to escape.

A handsome pup sat a distance away, watching us. He had a blaze on his muzzle, a white collar of fur, four white legs, and a white belly. He looked like a calendar picture of the classically marked Border collie.

I knelt down. "Here, pup."

He trotted over, head up, confident. I petted him.

A mostly black pup slunk back under the wagon. Mary and I leaned over and tried to coax him out. When I finally got hold of him, I noticed the roof of his mouth was black, a trait old-time sheepmen believed signified strong herding instinct. The minute I set him down, he dashed back under the wagon.

I reached for the shoe gnawer. Like the black pup, she was shy, and slipped under Roma's chair.

"Need a good dog to help with those sheep?" Roma asked.

I felt a pang. We'd had three stock dogs and all had come to bad ends. I didn't know if I had it in me to try again. But my eyes kept going to the poised pup who sat ten feet away, alternately studying me, Roma, Charlie, George, and Mary.

"If you're going to grow your business," Charlie said, "you just about have to have a good dog."

The stock dogs we'd lost all had shared a compulsive need to herd. That trait proved dangerous around cars. I'd worked to break them of chasing cars and kept them confined most of the time, but despite my carefulness, all had met with accidents involving vehicles.

It would be helpful to have a dog to pen sheep. Matt and Shane were good helpers, but sometimes I needed to move sheep when they were at school and George was at work. Mary knew how to corral sheep, but she would go to kindergarten next year. Besides, human help tired of running after sheep, but a good sheepdog believed it to be the greatest fun.

On top of that, we were trying to improve the cleanliness of our wool. Clean wool, uncontaminated by vegetable matter, brought more money. Hay and grain particles worked their way into the wool and had to be removed by hand at the woolen mill, so we tried to minimize how much feed fell onto their fleeces. But the ewes always beat me to the mangers, and I ended up tossing hay and grain onto their heads and backs.

"Could a dog keep the sheep back from the mangers when I'm feeding?" I asked.

"Of course," Charlie said.

"How?"

"The dog doesn't let the sheep eat until you say it's okay."

"But how do you train the dog to do that?"

Charlie looked puzzled. "You tell the dog not to let the sheep in."

"What I mean is . . ." I stopped. Kimball probably was one of those magical people whom animals obeyed naturally. Maybe he didn't know how to do it step-by-step.

Charlie said, "When you've got a good dog, you just tell it what you want it to do and it does it."

I nodded. I could get a video on training sheepdogs.

"My birthday is this week," I hinted to George.

"How much?" he asked Roma.

"Huh! I hope to God we're never so poor we have to charge people to get good dogs!" Roma stood firm on that and only with considerable urging accepted ten dollars to help with puppy food.

On the way home, the pup gazed out the window, sitting first on Mary's lap, then on mine. He showed no distress about leaving his mother and the home where he'd been raised. After awhile, he fell asleep between Mary and me.

When we returned home, Matt and Shane showered attention on the pup and took him off to show him the place.

I named him Duncan after Duncan in *Macbeth* because of his Scottish roots. On my birthday, Duncan endured wearing a party hat. When I blew out the candles on my cake, I made a wish that my new pup would avoid the tragedy that had befallen the others.

TWO

. . . .

At the time I met George I owned three sheep and a horse. When George picked me up for our first date and saw my three ewes in a pen, he stopped to look at them. George's grandparents, it turned out, had raised sheep in New Mexico, grazing bands of them on mountain pastures in the summer. George had experienced life as a sheepherder when he was ten years old. His mother and dad had sent him to a sheep camp to help tend his grandparents' flock. For months, his only human companions were Mexican herders who spoke no English except for the nickname they gave him, "Chicken Shit."

I had two other assets—five-year-old twin sons, Matt and Shane. I'd married their father, Chuck, during the Vietnam War. Chuck had lost his student deferment when he finished college. He went into the army. In boot camp, hobbling on blistered feet and with head ringing from the insults of drill sergeants, he called and asked me to marry him. Under everyday circumstances, we likely wouldn't have wed. The marriage lasted only a short time but produced a grand pair of boys.

The little boys and I had been on our own for a few years. I did magazine and newspaper writing, raised a garden, and had managed to hang on to my horse by way of a hay-for-writing arrangement.

A book contract had fallen my way, too, after an editor at Doubleday had seen a magazine article I'd written on western sheepherders. Following a hundred-year-old Rocky Mountain tradition, herders took bands of sheep to the mountains for summer grazing, then brought them back in the fall to winter in the valley. The editor believed their story worthy of a book.

That spring, I began my research by visiting lambing sheds. One day, as I was getting ready to leave a sheep ranch, the rancher put a bum (orphan) lamb into my arms and told me to take it home and raise it. The lamb had wide, innocent eyes and a sweet, distinctive smell. It peered up at me and said, "Maa-aa?"

The rancher said, "Careful. Sheep get in your hair." He was right. I raised another bum, then another.

"Nice ewes," George said on that first evening, gazing into their pen. No one else I'd dated had admired my sheep. He also greeted my Keeshond dog, Tundra, and Matt's cat, Peter.

I introduced George to Matt and Shane, then went to my bedroom to pick up a jacket. When I returned, George was on the floor with the boys and the three of them were laying out a board game. The babysitter fidgeted while I looked on, impressed.

George, a longtime bachelor, had streaks of gray in his hair but an easy, boyish smile. He was handsome, smart, and lived near Washington, D.C., where he worked as an engineer for the Department of Energy. He came to Idaho Falls, Idaho, periodically to check the progress of a small hydro power project. That's how I'd met him. I'd been doing public relations writing for DOE.

I enjoyed dinner with him, but at the end of that first evening, he astounded me by telling me he loved me. On our second date, he mentioned marriage. I felt attracted to him but thought he was rash. On the other hand, I remembered wonderfully romantic tales about enduring love that took root at first sight.

George suggested we get married around the first of the year. We would have known each other only a few months. Though we talked on the phone daily when he was in D.C., we had spent little face-to-face time together.

I expressed this doubt to George. He said, "I've waited too long already. I want a family."

I loved my life in rural Idaho. We had a small house, two lean-to animal shelters, and beautiful open spaces near our home. My neighbors, the Petersons, let the boys gather eggs at their house. We bought goat's milk from the Petersons and had fresh lamb for our table.

The little boys and I took long walks in lava fields near our house. On summer evenings we sat on the haystack, read books, pointed at hawks reeling overhead, and watched the sun paint colorful stripes onto the western horizon. I had plenty of social activities, but I longed for a full-time parenting partner to share the wonderfulness of my life. Plus, I knew firsthand how a child can long to have a dad in the home. I had never lived with my own dad, and my visits with him had been too short and too infrequent.

The next time George visited in Idaho, I asked about his parents. A coworker had told me that George had taken care of his mother when she was dying of cancer, so I asked about his father, who had died a long time before.

"Daddy," George said with his slight southern accent, "was the most admirable man in the world."

"Why?"

"He was always kind to everyone."

I chewed on this. This man had grown up with an example of kindness that he wanted to emulate. I turned his words over and over after I got home that night, and by morning, had turned a corner in my thinking.

George said we would marry and move to his home in Arlington, Virginia, only until he could swing a transfer, then we'd move back to Idaho and begin to raise sheep. While we were gone, farmer friends would keep my sheep and a rancher friend would put my horse to good use.

We said our marriage vows at my Episcopal church. Then George and I knelt at the altar and put our wrists together. My priest, Father Bob, wrapped them in his stole and intoned, "This symbolizes the three parties pledging to this marriage—George, Patti, and God." I gulped at the solemnity of it. My family held records for marital instability, but by God and with God, I'd do better.

At the reception, George's rancher cousin from New Mexico made an observation that showed he had an appreciation for dowry. Looking at Matt and Shane he said, "George got himself a couple of fine hands."

We had unseasonably good weather for our trip across the country and reached Virginia in time for me to enroll the boys in school before Christmas break ended.

The first morning in our new home, I went to the kitchen and searched for pots and pans. I looked outside and saw George sitting on the porch drinking a beer. It was 8 A.M.

"I'll be cooking breakfast," I said.

He lifted a can. "I've got mine."

But he came to appreciate food at breakfast time. He'd been a bachelor for so long, he gave me compliments on the simplest fare. One morning he asked, "What do you call this? It's delicious."

"That's, um, oatmeal."

Once a week, I took the subway into D.C. to visit museums. At first I said hello to fellow subway passengers and asked them how they were, but I received searing looks in return. Soon, like the others, I avoided eye contact and observed silence.

George's cat, Charley, resented us as intruders and bullied Matt's cat, Peter. Our easygoing, fluffy gray dog, Tundra, hated traffic and noise and became edgy.

A vacant lot overgrown with bamboo plants sat next to George's house and the boys played there, imagining jungle adventures. With George's help, they constructed a raft to float on a slow-moving creek a few miles from our house.

But in Idaho they'd had miles of empty land to explore. They had constructed roads and bridges to run trucks over, made forts from hay bales, dug underground forts, and had built a fire pit on the hillside.

One night I reached under Matt's pillow to retrieve the tooth he'd lost that day. I heard something rustle. I pulled out a sandwich bag that contained the tooth and a piece of notepaper. I went to the living room and turned on the light. In the Baggie, I found a careful drawing of a jet plane, with a note.

Dear Tooth Faree,
Would you plees bring me a jet plan so we can go back to Idaho?

The Baggie held pennies, dimes, and nickels. Matt understood that jets cost a lot, and a single tooth wouldn't purchase one.

I sat on the edge of the sofa, throat constricted. I, like Matt, longed for some magic. Could a request from a trusting, homesick child bring a supernatural solution our way so we could leave this crowded, unfriendly place?

The next day after school, I gave the boys a snack, then we put on coats and set off. If we could find a high vantage point, maybe we could see over the trees and buildings for a view of the setting sun.

We took a sidewalk that led upward, but when we got to the top of it, all we could see were trees and buildings, murky in the haze.

"We'll go higher," I said. Nearby, I saw a path in a small community park leading upward. We started up the hill. Dense tree growth surrounded us on both sides and birds sang. It wasn't Yellowstone Park, but it was pleasant. At the pinnacle of the path, we'd managed to get above the buildings. But the trees went on forever, and so did the gray film that obscured the sky. No sign of the sun.

"Should we go home?" Shane asked.

"Wait a minute." I looked around for a higher spot. I saw another rise. If we walked south a bit, then climbed . . . We started off again.

I felt like a madwoman. My ears and nose had gotten cold and the boys had grown tired of walking, but if I could see the sun hanging in the west where it belonged and watch it for just a few minutes, something inside me might be restored.

But it was not to be. To see above the trees and haze, we would have had to be in an airplane.

.   .   .

A priest at a local Episcopal church had lived for a while in Montana, and I remembered him saying he never forgot the experience. I called and asked if he'd have time to speak with me.

He listened sympathetically while I talked about my present life and how it differed from my former one. In Idaho I'd had trout fishing, trail riding, hiking, and wildlife. I put on my sunglasses when tears threatened.

"Mountain flowers don't transplant well," the priest said.

On weekends, we often took drives to the country. It took forever to get away from freeways with their dozens of traffic lanes and thousands of cars, but once we did, we found picturesque back roads with flowering trees and charming old homes. In Maryland, we drove past horse farms with white board fences and miles of green pasture. In Virginia, we found towns small enough to have grain silos and farm stores. In Delaware, George pointed out farms located within driving distance of the ocean.

"This would only be an hour-and-a-half commute for me," he said.

I tensed. Is that why we took weekend drives, to show me possible places to settle in the East?

I said nothing until the boys had fallen asleep in the backseat.

"Our plan said I'd come here until you could get a transfer. Then we'd go back to Idaho."

"We could find a place here."

"I don't like it here."

"I've always believed a person could be happy wherever she was, if she made up her mind to it."

We were back in city traffic. I gazed out the window at millions of headlights stretching into the distance. I searched for words but none came.

Soon something happened that helped me find my voice. I learned I was pregnant. I wanted our baby born where the air was clean and rivers ran wild, where a child had access to stars and sunsets.

In mid-August, I left Virginia so the boys could begin second grade in Idaho. George would come later. Though we left very early one morning, it already felt like a steam bath outside. Our shirts clung to us and our bare arms glistened with sweat. I tried to look solemn; I felt like squealing.

The boys and I camped our way across the country. Eastern campgrounds where we pitched our tent crawled with people, but when we got well past the Mississippi River, camping locations became more attractive. Tundra found places to run and became her wriggling, energetic self again.

When we reached the Idaho state line, I pulled our car onto the shoulder, got out, walked over, and grasped the "Welcome to Idaho" sign. I dropped to my knees. Matt asked in alarm, "What are you doing, Mom?"

I bent and kissed the ground. I didn't mean it as a joke.

Matt, Shane, and I settled back into our former routine while George made plans to join us. My sheep and horse came home. In the evenings I stood on the porch and gazed west. Sure enough, it was still there—the sun, falling onto the desert and creating a chaos of colors.

During phone calls over the following months, George and I talked about sheep breeds, feed costs, equipment needs, and where to locate a new lambing barn. We were eager to get on with raising sheep.

THREE

My *new pup made only one mess in the house.* After that, Duncan understood that matters related to personal plumbing needed to occur outside. The housebreaking success came about in part because I was well trained. I had no urgent writing deadlines, so I took him outside often.

But the housebreaking showed me how desperately Duncan wanted to please. Whenever I took him out to pee, I would praise him with an enthusiastic "Good dog!" when he relieved himself. After a couple of days, I noticed that when Duncan squatted, he locked eyes with mine to make sure I was watching. I also noticed that nothing came out. He liked praise so much, he pretended to pee. I was glad I noticed; otherwise I might have taken him inside right away, before we'd fulfilled our mission. As it was, it sometimes took five or six fakes before he actually accomplished anything.

His high sensitivity to criticism showed up early, too. If he jumped up on us, we told him, "No." If one of us made that "No" abrupt or loud, Duncan would shrink into a black-and-white ball, ears and tail dejected. I learned to say "No" in a matter-of-fact tone, and that was plenty of correction. But he really, really wanted to jump on people. He enjoyed greeting people and wanted to be acknowledged by them. His tense body told of his conflict. Welcome a person and get scolded? Follow the rules and miss out on being petted?

He came up with a compromise that allowed him to do both. Instead of jumping *on* someone, he would only jump near them. To accomplish this, he stood on his hind legs, offering his head at convenient petting height. He avoided putting his paws on the person. It was a credit to his agility that he could hang suspended beside a visitor for a considerable period of time. As a spirit-of-the-law person, I permitted this breach because Duncan really didn't intrude on visitors' space or get them dirty.

Herding, the trait unique to stock dogs, has been achieved through centuries of careful breeding and goes against a canine's natural instincts. Cattle and sheep could be prey to run down, but instead of harming livestock, stock dogs gather them.

My first stock dog had been Guernica, a pup whose heredity included three herding breeds. She bonded with me from the first day, and when only four months old, growled a threat at a male friend who greeted me with a hug. My dog trainer friend Lezlie warned, "Give her strong discipline or she'll run the farm."

Guernica learned basic obedience commands in the first couple of lessons. She loved to herd, and managed to keep children who played at our house bunched, something neighbor kids found strange but kind of fun. When not trying to pen children or the small number of sheep I had at the time, she stuck to me like lint. That is until she spotted a car coming down our gravel road. Then she dashed at it, nipping its tires as if they were the legs of cattle or sheep.

Lezlie, a gifted trainer, volunteered to help me break Guernica from chasing cars. We loaded our four preschool children into Lezlie's van, and Lezlie drove off. The van appeared a minute later at the crest of the road. I let Guernica off her leash. When she dashed out to chase the van, the kids hurled cans loaded with rocks, creating a terrible racket. Two of the cans struck Guernica, but she scarcely noticed.

"This calls for harsher measures." Lezlie disliked using force but hoped it would save Guernica's life. The next time that Guernica came abreast of the van, Lezlie opened the van's door. It knocked Guernica head-over-teacups into the ditch, but she came up without a blink and tore after the vehicle.

We'd used up Lezlie's best ideas. In most cases, Guernica wanted to mind, but where cars were concerned, an inner voice telling her to corral anything that moved prevailed over her good sense. I vowed to keep her tied when she was outside and next to me when I did chores. She normally hugged my leg anyway as I fed hay.

One morning she was trotting beside me when the school bus appeared on the hill. Her ears perked. "Guernica, no!" I scolded. She looked at me and her body squirmed. I could see in her face she wanted to obey, but the internal thing bred into her genes for hundreds of years overrode my command, and off she streaked. She was killed at only eighteen months old.

When Shane reached second grade, he wanted a dog for Christmas. George and I answered an ad in the paper advertising Australian shepherd/Border collie pups. We fell for a lovable brown-and-white pup with large, languorous eyes.

On Christmas morning, Shane walked slowly around the tree, looking for his present from Santa.

"Why don't you go outside and see if Santa left something for you in the yard?" George suggested.

"Santa doesn't do that!" Shane scowled, but went outside anyway and searched the snowy front yard. Then he glanced over and saw, standing on hind legs and peering out the window of the pickup, a pup wearing a red bow.

Shane rushed into the house, arms full of face-licking dog, yelling, "Santa brought me a puppy!" I'd recently read *Where the Red Fern Grows* to Matt and Shane, so Shane named his pup Dan after the coon dog in the book.

Dan knew he was Shane's pup. When Dan was only a few months old I could say to him, "Where is your boy?" and he would dive down the stairway to Shane and Matt's room, check on the beds, under them, and in the closet. If Shane wasn't there, he'd return upstairs with a worried look.

On school days Dan started watching for the school bus at 2 P.M. from atop the haystack. When it appeared, he would turn inside out with excitement. We saw that Dan had Guernica's tendency to chase cars with the intent of catching them, so he was seldom allowed to be free. He had a long chain that let him roam the yard and climb the haystack, and he was free to run with Shane and Matt on weekends. If a car came along, they grabbed hold of him.

George was doing chores one morning and loosed Dan to go with him to the barn. Like Guernica, Dan found the school bus irresistible, and was hit.

The vet gave us a discouraging prognosis, but we knew that dogs sometimes made miraculous recoveries, so we tried to save him. We fed him from a spoon and bathed the wounds on his disabled rear end. We kept his wooden box clean, changing and washing the rags and blankets we'd used to line it.

The days stayed warm and flies swarmed. It sickened us to find maggots in the open wounds on Dan's back. We immersed his rear end in warm water and solution.

We watched the dog shrink from a vigorous pup to a hank of hair and bones. Some days we felt encouraged, it seemed Dan's appetite was returning. But then we'd dress his wounds and see they had healed little.

Shane stopped participating in cleaning and dressing Dan's wounds. One day he said, "Let's not do this to him anymore."

We took Dan to the vet that afternoon. We buried him in our lower pasture and Matt and Shane marked his grave with an arrangement of toy trucks and rocks. Shane never again asked for his own dog.

Merlin came to us as a gift. A woman raising Kelpies, an Australian herd dog breed, had a six-month-old pup that hadn't sold, and she wanted it to go to a good home.

Merlin had a personality completely different from Guernica's and Dan's. I gave Merlin basic obedience training as I had the others, but with Dan and Guernica that had been rewarding. When I tried to teach Merlin to walk on a leash, he climbed the leash or flung himself on the ground. He refused to learn to sit, stay, or come.

He had an uncanny ability with sheep, however. During his first
month with us, I would go with him to bring in the sheep at night.
Later, I would simply say, "Merlin, go get the ewes," and he would
round them up and bring them to the barn by himself. After a short
time, he no longer had to be asked. He would stand at the door, telling
me it was time for him to gather the sheep.

"I ought to be grateful because Merlin is a valuable dog," I told a
friend. "But he's so hardheaded, I can't like him."

I saw meanness in him, too. One day when our faithful Keeshond,
Tundra, tried to eat from Merlin's dish, he grabbed her by the throat
and flung her to the ground. I had to drive him off with a broom.

Mary was a toddler, and I feared she might one day wander over
to Merlin's food. "He wouldn't hurt Mary," George said, but I stayed
watchful and fed Merlin in a corner of the yard away from the house.

While riding in the bed of the truck one day, Merlin flung himself
out to chase a dog going down the road. He must have tumbled a
long way, because when we retraced our route we couldn't find him.
Later, a vet's office called us—someone had found him in a borrow
pit, bleeding. He needed an expensive operation to amputate his leg.
We had him neutered at the same time. I hoped that now, with only
three legs and tame hormones, he would become manageable.

That didn't happen. One day when a neighbor boy was visiting,
Shane said, "Look how muscular this dog is," and ran his hands down
Merlin's back. Merlin turned and attacked Shane. I'd never seen a
bona fide dog attack before. Merlin lunged for Shane's throat. Because
of his missing leg Merlin lost his balance, but he came up snarling,
preparing to lunge again. George put out his leg and tripped the dog.

"That's it!" I announced, and looked around to see if anyone had
any argument. No one did. I put a leash on Merlin, took him to the
truck, and drove to the vet.

When I handed his leash to the receptionist I said, "Euthanize
him," and signed the paperwork.

"Would you like to stay?" she asked.

"We've had our good-byes." I drove away without a backward glance, with decisively dry eyes.

Matt, eleven, looked serious as a tree full of owls.

"Look." His black brows formed a **V** over his nose. He set the newspaper on the kitchen table and pointed to an article that listed the ten smartest dog breeds. Golden retriever was first, German shepherd second, sheltie third. Border collies hadn't even made the list.

"Where are Border collies?" Matt wanted to know.

"Maybe the list was put together by city people who don't know much about them."

Matt began to comb the article again. He would give the experts another chance. He walked off, face hidden by the paper.

Every year an article appeared listing the smartest dog breeds. The number one breed changed from year to year; one year Dobermans won the top spot, another year German shepherds, another year shelties. People who raised Border collies, a breed that originated in farm country between Scotland and England, had resisted joining the purebred dog community. Border collie breeders stressed intelligence and ability, while the American Kennel Club emphasized breed type and confirmation. Several U.S. breeds had become heavily inbred, developing weak hips and brains.

The American Kennel Club finally recognized Border collies as a breed in 1995, but the American Border Collie Association wanted none of it. The association pulled the papers of any Border collie registered with the AKC. The ABCA restricted their registration to pups whose parents came from working bloodlines. The association sponsored trials and events where Border collies got rewarded for doing what they had for hundreds of years—moving livestock from one place to another.

Eventually, the experts who generated the smart dog list put the Border collie in the top ten. In only a couple of years, it advanced to first place, and mostly has held that distinction since. Decades later, two Border collies, Rico and Betsy, would get international attention for their large vocabularies. Rico could understand 200 words, Betsy, 350. And Betsy appeared to be able to link photographs with the objects they represented, a skill researchers previously thought exclusively human.

But even before recognition came the Border collie's way, livestock raisers regarded their canine helpers as the cleverest dogs on the planet. They figured experts who failed to mention them on smart dog lists were the same guys who didn't know a heifer from a Hereford and who thought "wether" was a misspelling of "weather."

With Duncan, we once again had a clever herding dog. Duncan was smart and gentle, he loved to lure us into games, and he very much wanted to please. On top of that, I could see he had great promise with sheep.

But that characteristic also made me jittery. Strong herding instincts could mean an overwhelming desire to corral vehicles.

FOUR

....

While George still lived in Virginia, we talked often about which breed of sheep we'd like to raise. I suggested we might look seriously at the Polypay.

Polypay sheep had been invented in 1970 at the U.S. Sheep Station in Dubois, Idaho, fifty miles north of our farm. Researcher Dr. Clarence Hulet had a dream of developing a highly productive breed to supply quality protein for a protein-needy world. Sheep can graze areas of poor vegetation unsuitable for cattle and can go without water for long periods.

"Are you going to the fall sale at the sheep station?" George asked.

"I think so. They'll be selling Polypays, and I can look at them."

Dr. Hulet wanted to develop ewes that could breed out of season. Consumption of lamb in the U.S. had declined because lamb only appeared in supermarkets at certain seasons, and consumers got out of the habit of serving it. Dr. Hulet wanted to make lamb available year-round in stores.

Four established breeds went into making the Polypay: the Finnsheep, for high prolificacy, early puberty, and short gestation period; the Targhee, for size, long breeding season, and wool quality; the Rambouillet, for hardiness and wool quality; and the Dorset, a meat breed, for carcass quality, early puberty, heavy milking, and the ability to breed out of season.

Some raisers, especially range operators who grazed their flocks on U.S. Forest Service or Bureau of Land Management ground, scoffed at the station's new breed. They saw no advantage to having multiple-birth lambs; they believed a ewe could take care of only one lamb when she went to the hills.

Even some farm flock operators didn't like the idea of triplets and especially quadruplets. "If a ewe produces too many multiples," a woman told me, "the operator ends up raising a lot of sheep on bottles and that doesn't pay."

But one neighbor, a longtime sheep raiser, combed over the sheep station literature and announced he thought the Polypay was the best breed ever created.

So on a bright September morning I drove off to Dubois (pronounced "Doo-boys") to investigate the new breed. Trucks with stock racks and trucks pulling horse trailers filled parking lots surrounding the sale barn. I walked up and down the aisles of sheep, looking at various breeds before coming to pens of Polypay ewes and ewe lambs. The Polypays had sweet, open faces like sheep pictured in a child's illustrated Bible. But cuteness shouldn't influence me.

I moved to two large pens of Polypay rams.

"See one ya like?" a tall old man asked me.

"I don't know what I'm looking for."

"Ya know much about the Polypay?"

"I've been reading about them, but these are the first I've seen."

"They're gonna revolutionize this industry."

"Do you have some?"

"I do. I'm phasing out my other breeds."

"You must not have a range outfit."

"I do. I run my sheep on forestland and the Polypays are doing great. If a ewe takes two lambs to the mountains, she comes home with two. If she takes triplets, she comes home with all three. They're wonderful mothers and easy to herd." He pushed back his hat. "Get in there and feel 'em. I think you'll be surprised."

Though pregnant, I was still agile. I climbed over the fence and walked among the milling sheep, trying to look knowledgeable.

"You know which one I'd pick?"

"No."

"That one right there." He pointed.

"Why?"

"He's skinny and not much to look at now. But you know how a skinny kid often turns out better than one who develops early?"

I didn't, but I said, "Yeah."

"He'll grow out real good. And because he's not big and impressive, buyers won't notice him and he won't go for too much money. Let me check his wool." Dr. Hulet had considered wool quality in his dream breed, too, to give sheep raisers a second cash crop.

The man got in, took hold of the ram, and plucked out some wool. He looked at it closely, then handed it to me.

"Hmm," I said.

"Pretty nice, huh?"

"Don't you want him?"

"I'm not buying rams today. I'm buying ewes."

I thanked the rancher, wrote down the ram's number, and whispered to it, "Do you want to come live at our house?" The ram lifted his chin and gazed into my eyes, then moved closer to me. No serious livestock buyer would believe in omens, but I thought I'd seen one.

Before long, station employees came to the barn with herd dogs to start moving the sheep through chutes to the sale barn. When a sheep balked and wouldn't go farther, a dog would leap onto its back and urge it to keep moving.

The rancher had predicted accurately. Two other bidders started out trying to get "my" ram but dropped out, and the ram sold to me. Because I'd driven up in the car, I made arrangements to come back the next day with the truck to get him.

George called that night. "I've been at the Virginia State Fair today, and guess where I ended up hanging around?"

"The sheep barn," I guessed.

"Right. Guess what breed we're going to raise?"

"Uh-oh."

"Suffolks! I had a long talk with a Suffolk raiser, and they're great sheep. Big, meaty, and fast-growing."

"Um, sounds impressive."

"What?"

"I bought a Polypay ram today. An old rancher came by and gave me good help. And we'd been leaning that way, right?"

After a minute he laughed. "Then, it's Polypays." He wondered, "How many sheep will we want?"

"I think when we get to fifty ewes, we'll feel like we have a 'real' flock."

We were on our way.

George found a job in Idaho Falls and moved home before our baby girl was born. In addition to that considerable joy, we now had pens of Polypay ewes getting ready to lamb. Because Idaho is the gem state, we named our first Polypays after gems. The ram I'd bought became Jasper, and we named ewes Opal, Ruby, Lapis Lazuli, Sapphire, Pearl, Emerald, Agate, etc. A purebred flock made sense for an operation our size. We could select for wool quality, productivity, heavy milking, and good dispositions. Customers would be willing to pay above-market prices to get stock that would improve the genetics of their commercial flocks, or they might want to start purebred operations of their own.

We owned five acres of land already and bought forty more from a farmer. We fenced five acres of it for sheep pasture. We kept only ewes that lambed twins at one year of age. We weighed lambs to see how well their mothers were milking and sold off ewes that didn't meet our standards, but even so, it didn't take us long to get to fifty ewes. A real flock.

I worried every time I took Duncan outside. He couldn't be on a leash and work as a sheepdog, but I knew from sad experience how quickly a dog could dash away and meet with disaster.

So I undertook a stringent training program. Few cars came down our dirt road, so I took him to the nearby paved road where cars came by with some regularity, three or four an hour, along with an occasional speeding potato truck or lumbering combine.

Sure enough, and to my dismay, vehicles intrigued Duncan. When a vehicle came near, he would drop to his belly, preparing to do the Border collie sneak, a maneuver where he would creep slowly forward, giving the animal he intended to move "the eye."

When Duncan responded to a car this way, I jerked his choke collar and told him "*No!*," not caring if I hurt his feelings. I hoped his ambition to chase sheep wasn't being thwarted and that he could discern between this situation and the work asked of him in the sheep pens. After a few of these walks on the road, he would look at me first, yearningly, when he saw a vehicle approaching. I could see it was a terrible struggle for him not to drop to his belly, and sometimes he didn't resist.

"Have you tried lifting him and shaking him?" my friend DeeDee asked. She'd read an article that said for big, life-threatening issues, a handler could employ the stern method mother dogs use. Pick the pup up by the skin on his back and shake him soundly.

I had my chance the next time Duncan and I were on the road. When he saw a car coming, he started to drop to a crouch. I picked him up by the skin, shook him hard, and said, "*NO!*" He looked astonished.

Before we finished our walk, another car came along. Duncan pretended he didn't see it. Whether it was the shaking or the earlier lessons or both, Duncan started averting his eyes when a car approached. It was comical how he gazed off at the fields looking determinedly blasé.

Discouraging him from chasing horses became part of his training, too. "*No!*" I'd tell him when he'd creep into their corral. If horses were standing quietly, Duncan could resist their pen, but when horses were running and playing and bucking, he couldn't contain himself and would dash after them, barking, insisting that order be restored. I didn't put horses and cars in the same danger category; a horse

could kick him, but he was so agile and swift it seemed unlikely. So I
worked on that aspect of his training more gradually.

Mary came to me one day holding a pink jelly shoe, shredded.

"Duncan?" I tried to match Mary's disappointed expression, but
I hadn't liked those flimsy shoes anyway.

"You need to scold him!"

"I will." Duncan wanted to please, but had the puppy inclination to
chew. I reminded myself of that when I found him growling, shaking
the garden hose in his teeth. When I turned the hose on, it spouted
leaks. Never mind, I told myself, we have lots of hoses. But when I un-
wound two others that had been hanging in the barn, they, too, had
been punctured by puppy teeth. I began totaling in my head the cost of
replacement hoses.

"Duncan!"

He ears waved like flags, and he grinned. He thought we were going to play or maybe go to the pasture and visit sheep.

"You need to stop chewing up everything! You have chew toys
and bones all over."

Later that day, I found a new tennis shoe of mine completely destroyed. I'd worn the pair only twice.

"Duncan!" I scolded.

His ears drooped. But I knew he didn't get the drift. Chewing
came too natural to a pup. We embarked on a program to keep anything of value out of reach.

Poor, aging Tundra, our Keeshond, saw Duncan as the pup from
hell. He pulled Tundra's ears, barked and yapped at her, dashed in and
bit her, ran circles around her. He figured out her every hiding place.
Sometimes I shut her in the back bedroom just to give her a break.

For Tundra, all the pups had been a nightmare. Guernica had kept
Tundra away from me, Dan had been a general annoyance, and Merlin had shown an angry, dangerous side. Duncan proved the most
energetic and insistent.

Duncan probably extended Tundra's life by a few months because his harassment forced her to get exercise. For a while, she ate better and seemed less stiff. But the interruption in her decline didn't last. When complete blindness and deafness had taken away her quality of life, we made a decision.

George and I drove Tundra to the vet. This time, of course, I wanted to stay until the end. As we petted her gray coat and thanked her for years of sweetness and loyalty, she slipped away.

We buried her in the backyard. Matt and Shane, now ten years old, made a grave marker of colorful rocks and wildflowers, and on a cross they built from lumber scraps wrote, "She Has Gone Where She Won't Suffer Anymore."

When we'd come back from the vet with the dead Tundra, lively Duncan had greeted us. Worries for his survival had helped me keep a bit of emotional distance from him. But now with Tundra gone, Duncan's charm, plus his willingness to abandon an interest in cars, proved irresistible. Any remaining detachment melted away.

FIVE

....

My longtime friend Mel drove out from town to join Duncan and me for a walk. Mel, whose daughters babysat for me, loved the outdoors, plus we shared an interest in spiritual topics. We often discussed serious subjects as we walked.

We chose a path beside fields of blooming alfalfa. When the farmland ended, we wove our way through sagebrush up a lava hillside. Though only a hundred feet higher than surrounding land, the hill offered a restful view of farms below and mountains to the east and south.

Mel and I stepped carefully around stinging nettle, crawled onto a lava outcrop, and sat down. Duncan investigated scents in the brush. I reached for a tissue and blew my nose.

"You have another cold," Mel noted.

I nodded.

"Do you ever ask yourself why you get so many colds?"

"I get so many colds," I said, hoping annoyance didn't come through in my words, "because I'm around little kids."

Mel looked at me, expressionless.

"Little kids have a lot of germs and adults who are around them pick up a lot of stuff." Surely, she must know this. Still, she said nothing. My irritation rose. Yet, I saw concern on her face, too, and that made me scold myself for bristling.

"I'm very busy," I said.

"I've noticed. What's that about?"

"It's about—I have a lot to do. Writing, the sheep, the horses, 4-H, soccer, the food bank, driving kids to lessons."

Mel didn't answer.

"It's lucky I'm energetic." Breakfast had been hours before, but something undigested churned in my stomach.

Mel's face stayed neutral. Finally she smiled into my eyes and said in a kind voice, "Do you think it might be good to look at your busyness and your colds on your own, before life forces you to?"

Mel believed sickness had emotional roots. I did, too, actually, but she took it further than I. She thought when people refused to look at their emotional pain they got more pain, in the form of illness. I'd had pain, I suppose, in my growing-up years. When I recalled those years— infrequently and to myself—I could see a lot had been abnormal, but I consoled myself with the knowledge those turbulent years hadn't hurt me. All I had to do was look at my present life to know that. I'd married a smart man, I had three delightful children, and we lived a pleasant, rural life surrounded by animals.

A person could choose whether to allow a troubled childhood to follow her into adult life, and I'd chosen not to. I couldn't say how colds worked for others—whether they had emotional causes—but in my case, a cold was just a cold.

SIX

....

Duncan was so eager to work, it was hard to postpone trying him on useful chores, yet I didn't want to ask too much of him when he was only six months old. But one day when I was carrying an armload of hay, the sheep stampeded me and nearly knocked me over. When I got to the mangers, I dumped the hay and watched it splash like rain onto their wool.

Maybe I could try Charlie Kimball's suggestion about getting Duncan to keep the flock back. If it proved too much for him or if he created terrible chaos, I would delay a second try for a few more months.

Feeling silly, at the next feeding I sat down on the haystack with him, put my arm around him, and did what Kimball had suggested. "I have a problem, Dunc, and I hope you can help me with it."

He tilted his ears forward.

"It would be better for me and better for the wool if the sheep didn't swarm me."

His face went solemn.

"Do you think you could shoo them off until I've finished putting out hay?"

His mouth fell open in a smile.

"Okay, let's go try."

Duncan could go into the sheep pens only with permission. "Come on," I said, and Duncan flew over the fence. He looked at me. What next?

"Shoo 'em," I said.

Maybe it wasn't the talk I'd had with him. Maybe I conveyed what I wanted psychically, or maybe I told him with body language. Whatever the reason, Duncan, young dog that he was, dashed into the midst of the sheep. Older, big ewes didn't want to give way to a pup, but he ran at them individually, forcing them to back up.

I wanted to quit there on a successful note but decided to push on. "Keep them back, Duncan," I said. Incredibly, he did. Scarcely believing how easy it was, I filled feeders with hay while Duncan ran back and forth, forcing the complaining, blatting sheep to stand back. From that day, Duncan went into the pens with me whenever I fed.

The sheep still managed to toss hay around when they were eating and some of it went into their wool, but feeding had become pleasant. Instead of being mobbed, I calmly deposited portions of hay while Duncan kept ewes behind an imaginary line. I felt sorry for him; it required so much running and concentration to make sure no ewe busted through. But I learned how much he enjoyed his new job when I was talking to a friend on the phone.

"I've taught Duncan to 'shoo' the sheep," I said.

Duncan dashed to the back door, ears perked, with a hopeful look on his face. He moaned to be let out.

We learned the command "Shoo" could not be used in conversation at risk of disappointing Duncan. If we said "Shoo," and didn't intend to do it right away, Duncan became crestfallen; his ears fell and his body slumped. If we were working sheep in the barn and I said, "Should I call Duncan in to shoo the sheep?" he would suddenly materialize and sail over the fence into the midst of them. The word took on a reverence, said twice a day as a command, the rest of the time spelled out, S-H-O-O.

Amazingly, Duncan could distinguish homonyms. He never once thought he was about to go to work when someone said, "I can't find my other shoe."

I'd stopped worrying so hard about losing Duncan to a mishap with a car. But danger, I learned, could lurk in unexpected places. I was co-leader of my kids' 4-H Livestock Club. Four-H, an organization originally aimed at rural kids, had expanded to include urban interests like science and technology, but our club reflected the earlier purpose—raising animals, and developing responsibility and good citizenship.

Each year in spring, our 4-H club took baby animals to a local nursing home. Deirdre, the activities director, refused to worry about messes on the sparkling floor and cheerfully followed us around with a roll of paper towels. Many of the residents had been raised on farms or had farmed until retirement, and Deirdre believed messes were a small price to pay for the pleasure farm animals gave the old people.

When we arrived with rabbits and chickens in cages, baby pigs or lambs in arms, we created a stir, and residents came back from wherever they had escaped to.

An old woman tied in a wheelchair, head fallen on her chest, managed to recognize the clucking of chickens. Her head came up and her feeble eyes tried to find the source of the sound. Jeanette, one of our 4-H'ers, carried her cage of chickens over to the old woman, lifted the woman's hand into the cage, and helped her stroke a white hen. The old woman nodded. Jeanette spent a long time with the woman, chattering about her chickens and their individual personalities.

The piglets squealed at ear-deafening pitches and pooped simultaneously, as if their squealers and bowels were connected. I hoped Deirdre would order us not to bring pigs back, but she didn't. She only grinned as old people smiled at the piglets, petted their bristly sides, and cooed, "Are you the one who had roast beef?" Or, "Don't build your house out of straw, ha-ha!" After a certain length of time, the pigs ran out of rank-smelling poop, and then I felt easier about them.

The lambs were perennial favorites. In all the years we took lambs, I never saw one make a mess while a 4-H'er carried it around to visit with residents. I and other parents worried that the hooves of a wriggling lamb might scrape the parchment-thin skin of a resident or, if it kicked, inflict bruises that wouldn't heal. But our 4-H'ers had no such concerns.

"Would you like to hold it?" Nick, a blond boy with an armful of lamb, asked a frail old lady.

"Yes, I would. Put it right here in my lap."

The lamb sat quietly, innocent lamb eyes gazing at the white ceiling, head against the woman's bony bosom. Did the animals know to be careful? Or maybe we were just lucky.

Duncan was still young, about seven months old, when he first went with us to the nursing home. Matt led him on a leash, and the two had barely stepped into the lobby when a stately old man spotted the dog.

"Border collie," he breathed. The old man sat down in a chair and waited for Duncan to come to him. Duncan led Matt to the old man, sat down between the man's knees, and gazed up politely. The conversation took place between the old man and Duncan, though Matt had to supply some answers.

"Aren't you a swell dog? I bet you're good help."

"He is. He's smart."

"I can tell by the look of you. Is it sheep you work, or cattle?"

"Sheep."

"I used to have sheep and wonderful dogs to help me. Dolly was the best. When we started raising cattle, Dolly helped me just as much with the cows. What's your name?"

"Duncan."

"That's a fine name. I'm pleased to meet you. Do they take good care of you, Duncan?"

"They do. Er, we . . ."

Other kids had brought dogs—a pug and another Border collie—and some had brought cats. Residents gathered around the dogs and cats and made conversation with the kids.

"What's your dog's name?"

"How long you had that tabby cat?"

"Lookie here. A blue-eyed cat. Where'd you get it?"

The men and women who'd been ranchers were drawn to the Border collies like ants to frosting. They told stories of their former herd dogs, stretching the accomplishments of the dogs.

But it wasn't all a Norman Rockwell scene between the young and the old. The messes and unpleasant odors didn't all come from the animals. One old man with yellowed skin leered over the French door of his room and announced in graphic language what he'd like to do to the visiting mothers and girls. A plump mom muttered, "Fat chance, Grandpa. You ain't had work in that field for thirty years."

When we'd finished visiting the main part of the facility, Deirdre asked who might want to go to the Alzheimer's unit. Our entire group gamely followed her to another wing. Understandably, residents there were less responsive. But eager children insisted on putting poultry, piglets, and lambs in the old people's view. Patients gave little indication they knew the animals or kids were there, but Deirdre said to me, "Who knows how cut off they really are? We can at least try."

One elderly man sat in a chair staring into space. His daughter who was visiting spied the Border collies.

"Oh, Dad, look!" she said. "Dogs like you had."

The man seemed to try to focus—not his eyes as much as his mind.

"Would you like to hold this dog?" Matt offered.

Matt placed Duncan in the man's lap. I wondered if Duncan would try to jump down, but he sat perfectly still. The man's stiffened hand came up like a claw and stroked the pup's head. Suddenly, the man emitted a moan. "Oh God." He hugged the pup to him. "Oh God!" He began to cry. His fingers tightened around the dog's neck.

His daughter reacted immediately. "Dad! That's too hard." She tried to uncoil the man's fingers. His cries got louder and he clutched tighter. "Oh my God!" he sobbed.

The daughter looked to Deirdre, who came over to help. A nurse hurried over, too.

"No, darlin'," the nurse ordered, trying to pry the man's hands loose. "Let go!" The nurse and Deirdre struggled against the man's grip. Duncan started to gasp.

"Can I help?" I asked, meaning, "Hurry!"

"Oh, oh, oh!" the man wept.

Duncan eyes got round and an awful noise came from his throat.

I tried to pull back one of the man's fingers to give Duncan space to breathe.

When Deirdre and the nurse had successfully loosened the man's grip, I scooped up Duncan. He wheezed, shook his head, and blinked.

Children rushed over. "Duncan. Are you all right?"

"Duncan, would you like a glass of water?"

The man's daughter, who looked shipwrecked, said, "I'm so sorry."

I asked Deirdre, "What do you think Duncan called up in the man's mind?"

"If I were to guess, I'd say loss."

A parent said, "Good thing that was Duncan. Most any other dog would have scratched and bit." It had happened so fast, I hadn't thought to worry about the old man and his wafer-thin skin.

Driving home later, I looked at Duncan settled in the backseat between Matt and Shane, his head resting on his paws, looking none the worse for his ordeal. When he was being choked, I'd seen concern in his eyes but no panic. I think he understood everyone was working to free him.

I'd seen something else, too. What it would be like to be Duncan's person. Though he'd stick to me like foxtail seed, I would be sharing him with the larger world.

SEVEN

"What do you need money for?" George took off his glasses and set them on the table. He was paying bills, so I'd thought it a good time to interrupt him with a question about money.

"We're going on a trip and I'd like to have some pocket money."

"We're just going camping. There won't be any place to buy things."

"We'll go to town at some point and I might want to buy a souvenir?" I disliked that my voice sounded thin. Only a few years before, all financial decisions had fallen to me. Even as a teenager, I'd held jobs that allowed me to buy clothes and school supplies, and after high school, I'd worked and lived on my own while attending night classes. It was weird to be asking George for money in case I wanted a souvenir.

"If you see something you like, all you have to do is ask for it." George gave me a reassuring smile.

I thought about it. I no longer had to write checks to utility companies, study bank statements, or read insurance policies. George didn't answer when I asked him how much money he made or what amount we were putting into savings, but he didn't balk at giving me money for family expenses.

All things considered, I had it good. I got to write, have fun with the kids, and work with animals. And I didn't have to worry about the hassles of money.

"We need one of these." George pointed at the farm catalog and a mesh contrivance called a sheep chair, used for trimming hooves. We trimmed hooves, which are like human toenails, in spring and fall,

because if hooves got too long, the sheep's foot became susceptible to disease and lameness.

We'd been using a labor-intensive method of setting the ewe on her rump, then I would hold her around the neck while George used hoof trimmers on her. I often got hit by flailing hooves or a tossing head while George got kicked by thrashing feet and cut by the trimming tool.

When our sheep chair arrived, we couldn't wait to try it. We hung it on the top board of a wooden panel in the barn and I told Duncan, "Go get the sheep."

Duncan's ears went up like flags. He wagged, then dashed out of the barn. From the barn door, we watched him run to the end of the field and begin circling the sheep. He dropped to his belly and gave them the eye, and the ewes started moving toward the barn.

He brought them to the outside pen, and herded them into it. A couple ewes turned and ran back toward the field, but speedy Duncan intercepted them and lunged at their heads. They changed direction and raced back to the pen.

Mary and Matt stationed themselves beside the aisle we'd made of wooden panels, to urge ewes forward. Shane manned the temporary gate we'd made, and he let out one sheep at a time. Grabbing the ewe around the neck, George backed her into the chair.

The ewe looked comical when seated, like she might be ready to settle in with a book. But the chair immobilized her so she couldn't struggle or flail. Hoof trimming had gone from being an event that tested tempers to being a fairly easy Saturday morning chore.

Sheep shearing remained the big springtime challenge. It was difficult to find shearers, because the few men practicing the trade favored large operations. So we threw in with our neighbors, Doris and Elwood Kirby, Suffolk raisers. They hosted a joint shearing in their fine old barn.

We walked our sheep down to their place. Shane rode the dependable Lucy, flanking the sheep on their left. Matt rode the sweet-natured but occasionally energetic Rainbow, flanking the sheep on their right.

George, Mary, and I walked behind; Duncan ran a wide circle around all of us.

We had little concern our sheep would bolt and try to go very far. White-faced sheep like ours had been bred to stay together. Black-faced sheep, like the Suffolk, came from sparsely vegetated places where it was desirable for them to spread out. We would have been much busier herding Suffolks.

Still, we didn't want our sheep straying into yards. Our country mile had only a few houses, but we didn't want our sheep nibbling on neighbors' tulips.

When we neared the Kirbys', Shane rode ahead and blocked the road. Our sheep turned into the Kirbys' driveway as though they'd been going there for years.

Elwood Kirby watched Duncan circling the sheep. The dog kept his collie eye sharp for any ewe that might try to escape and go home. The ewes watched Duncan, too, always aware of his whereabouts.

"Mighty good dog," Elwood said.

The Kirbys had set up a holding pen in their barn and had swept an area of floor clean for shearing. A couple of the Kirby grandchildren were bringing ewes into the barn. When one of the Suffolks balked, Duncan lunged at her. The big ewe whirled on him, stomped her foot, lowered her head, and charged. Duncan, quick as a rabbit, dodged, but he looked astonished. He wasn't used to such independence and size.

The shearer spread a tarp on the floor and plugged in his shearing equipment. Despite the benefit of motorized equipment and a protective waist belt, the sheep shearer would put in a backbreaking day, holding each animal between his legs and rotating it as he sheared so the fleece would come off in one piece. After the shearer finished the first ewe, his helper folded the fleece in the prescribed way and tied it into a bundle with paper ties. Polypropylene twine was forbidden because its small fibers worked their way into sheep wool and had to be removed by hand at woolen mills. Only string made from natural fibers was allowed at a shearing.

The Kirbys had hung long burlap wool sacks from the roof beams and the shearers tossed fleeces into them. When the bag got half full Elwood called, "Where are the sheep stompers?"

Matt and Shane stopped forward. We'd told them the job of stomper would fall to them.

George picked up Shane and dropped him into the burlap wool sack. Shane started jumping up and down. When he'd packed down the wool, George helped him get out. Next time, it was Matt's turn. After the sack was tightly packed, Elwood sewed the mouth of it shut with paper twine.

"Look." Matt showed me a red insect crawling on his arm. It was a sheep tick, not a true tick, but nevertheless a nasty, crawly pest. Fortunately for Matt and Shane, the Kirbys' sheep and ours were mostly tick-free.

Shearing took only a couple of minutes per ewe, so in just a few hours we were on our way home with naked, blue-white sheep that had lost a lot of size. I could recognize individual ewes when they had fleeces, but without their coats I had to strain to tell them apart.

Mature ewes, frisky with their heavy coats gone, jumped straight into the air or butted heads for fun. Duncan had to run harder to keep them in line.

George and I ambled at the rear, content to let Duncan do the worrying. Mary rode in the saddle with Shane.

"I don't remember being involved in shearing time when my grandparents had sheep." In George's family, the sheep had belonged to his maternal grandparents.

"Did your dad help with them?"

"Not much. He didn't get along with Grandmother."

"Why not?"

"She thought he was a bum. The drinking, mostly. After he shot himself, she—"

"Wait! I thought your father died in a hunting accident."

George gazed up at the afternoon sun. "He hoped it would look like an accident. But we came to see it was intentional."

"But you—" I stopped. This didn't seem a subject for cross-examination. "He was depressed?"

"He and Mama had split up, maybe for the last time."

"They split up a lot?"

"He went on binges and would be gone for months. Then he'd return."

"What did your mother do?" I probably should have tiptoed around this subject, but I couldn't help wanting to know more.

"She always took him back. While he was gone, she held things together. She had a job at the courthouse and kept food on our table."

George had told me his father was the kindest man he'd ever known. But deserting a family and leaving his wife holding the bag didn't sound kind at all.

Duncan dashed after a too-frisky yearling who had spotted a delicious lilac bush. He pushed her back with the others.

"What would he do when he came home?"

"Look for a job. Stay sober for a while."

"Did he stay away long?"

"Sometimes for months." He sounded as if it were a normal thing.

"Did you hear from him?"

"No. Daddy never let us know where he was."

"You must have worried."

"Yeah." After a minute he said, "I think Mama wasn't going to take him back that last time, and that's why he shot himself."

I blinked against the sun and pulled down my hat brim.

"We were lucky to get in with that shearer," George said. "He told Elwood he's booked up solid for the next month and a half."

It was clear we had changed the subject, but my mind had a hard time returning to the topic of finding shearers.

The next fall, George decided to become our shearer. He took a week's leave from work and went to sheep-shearing school. He won the belt buckle for being best student.

EIGHT

Our March lambing brought us an abundance of multiple births. Selecting for high productivity was working; sixty percent of our ewes had quadruplets. Even first-time lambers had triplets.

They all lambed within a few weeks, too. That shortened the time we had to get up in the night to check ewes, but the barn overflowed with ewes and their litters. We made makeshift jugs in the middle of the barn, and when we did chores, had to crawl over panels to deliver food and water, an additional expenditure of energy during an already exhausting time.

We supplemented our quad lambs with bottle feedings, delivering powdered milk supplement to the lambs four times a day. The kids pitched in to help when they weren't at school, but George and I grew ever wearier from the demands in the barn.

By late spring, the workload had lightened. We hadn't had much moisture during the winter, so we started watering our alfalfa fields in May. That's when Duncan discovered ballet.

Duncan loved his work in the sheep pens and we regarded him as indispensable. That might seem like fulfillment enough for any individual, but Duncan found a way to express himself artistically, too.

All summer, until early fall, we watered our fields with river water, which came to us via a canal system. Matt and Shane carried long sticks of pipe, called hand lines, from one setting to the next, a job that gave them summer wages, flexible hours, and a determination to go to college so they wouldn't have to perform such labor later in life.

Each pipe had three nozzles—one on either end and one in the middle. The nozzles moved 360 degrees, broadcasting a circle of water. We left the water on for twelve hours, then Matt or Shane would move the lines to the next location.

For Duncan, it was love at first sight. The first time he watched water spew out of the nozzles, his ears went to hyper-alert position. He stood transfixed, watching the fountains and listening to the rhythmic *chig, chig, chig* of water moving in an arc. His body quivered with excitement. Then he streaked away, heading toward an end nozzle.

When he reached it, he leaped into the air, trying to catch a stream of water. He fell back to earth, graceful as a snowflake, then ran to the next nozzle. When he got close to it and its spouting water, he did a *grand jeté*, hung suspended, then let himself float back to earth.

At the next nozzle, he pointed himself at the water, folded his front legs as he sailed upward, arched his neck, and bit the water as he floated past. He found dainty feet just as he touched down.

From the start he was a natural, but he became more impressive with practice. I regretted we didn't have a video camera to record his performances. But Duncan did not dance for show. Like any real artiste, he did it for his own enjoyment. When he was dancing in the water, he was totally consumed, aware of nothing beyond the cascading spray. In most any activity Duncan showed a high level of delight, but when dancing with sprinklers, he was the embodiment of joie de vivre.

He put variety into his irrigation dances, too. One time he would execute a *tour en l'air*, leaping from a crouching position and making a complete circle before touching down. Another time he would jump sideways to follow a spray, his legs bent at the knees, toes neatly pointed. Another time he would race at the approaching stream, launch himself into the midst of it, spiral, and land gracefully. Another time he would hurl himself at a stream that already had gone past, spiraling from the moment he took off. He added drama to his performance by flinging his muzzle at the spray before he fluttered back to earth.

I loved to chop vegetables or load the dishwasher when the sprinklers were running. My kitchen window looked out at the back field.

I could watch the beautiful Duncan, delicate and airy as Margot Fonteyn, strong and expressive as Rudolf Nureyev. He would get soaked, of course, and his black coat would become heavy with water. It might seem like it'd be hard for him to look impressive soaked and skinny, but the minute he went airborne, grace overcame absurdity.

Sometimes company arrived at our house and left again without Duncan even noticing them. I wondered that he didn't get tired. He would travel from one end of the field to the other, then back again, hours at a time. If we really needed Duncan at the house, I could call him away from the sprinklers and he would return. But I didn't do this often. Art should not suffer interruption.

The artificial rain gave Duncan a wonderful physical workout and hours of enjoyment. Real rain did not deliver the same pleasure. It might have, if real rain hadn't been accompanied by thunder and lightning. Thunder terrified him, and even distant lightning sent him into hiding. Perhaps his keen ears could hear thunder no matter how far away it was, or maybe he linked lightning streaks to approaching thunder. I suspect his hearing was hypersensitive, because he hated summer fireworks, too.

He disliked the approach of storms as much as he disliked storms themselves. Duncan could prophesy the weather with dead-on accuracy. He became miserable the moment he perceived a storm on the way. Changes in barometric pressure or the ions must have alerted him. Then the happy, confident dog would disappear and a morose, tense creature would replace him. He would slink to the porch, moaning and whimpering, bang his paw against the door, and plead to be admitted.

He got wind of a storm so early, it was easy to dismiss his worries. "Duncan, go away! There's no storm around." But I came to see he was infallible. The sky overhead could be a bowl of uninterrupted blue, with no wisp of cloud anywhere, but if Duncan showed up on the porch, head and tail tucked, eyes round with apprehension, it meant a storm was coming, even if six hours away.

This gave me a way to have fun with my town friends. I would tell

Ronna or DeeDee. "It looks like the weather is going to change in the next few hours."

"What are you talking about?" they would say. "It's a perfect day. The TV weatherman said it will be sunny for the next two days."

"We farm folks can tell weather changes better than meteorologists. We watch which way the ants are walking and that tells us all we need to know." Certain as taxes, a few hours later, dark clouds would replace the sunshine and the sky would start to rumble.

But I would have preferred not to have this insider's look at the weather. It was tough to watch Duncan, full of dread, shaking like a palsied old man.

Our best attempts to reassure him failed. He sought an inside wall as far from windows as he could manage. That was Matt's closet. Matt would open his closet door for Duncan when he came pleading. Matt's collection of dirty clothes, magazines, shoes, socks, and assorted papers offered Duncan a place where he could nose under debris to hide from the storm. But that sanctuary didn't satisfy Duncan for long. Then he would slink to Matt's bed, trembling. Matt would suspend our rule about dogs staying off furniture and invite Duncan to join him. Arm around Duncan, Matt would continue reading. But Duncan would whine, moan, stand, circle, tremble, jump off the bed, jump back on, and finally slink off to find another hiding place, stealing past windows, ducking under furniture, searching for a place where he would have no reminder of the flashing skies. But no such place existed.

One night he practically came into the shower looking for me. When I heard him scratching, I reached over and opened the bathroom door. He ran in, put his front feet on the bathtub rim and poked his head into the spray. "Storm coming!" his alarmed look said.

His behavior became most distressing in the middle of the night. Duncan often stayed on the porch or in the garage on summer evenings, but when a thunderstorm was coming, he wanted in. One of us would hear him whine and go admit him.

Duncan sought my side of the bed. He would put his head on my pillow and moan into my ear. When the first streak of lightning came, he would emit an agonized cry. Then he would crawl behind the headboard, running amok of cords connected to lamps, clocks, and the radio. A moment later, the black muzzle would be back, an inch from my face. I felt sorry for him and tried to console him for the first thirty minutes. After that, my patience wore thin.

"Duncan, stop! I want to go to sleep."

Idaho's summer thunderstorms often lasted for hours. Particularly at night, the pyrotechnics could be spectacularly beautiful, but not for a person whose dog was yowling an inch from her face. Usually once or twice during a summer, lightning would hit near our house. The noise that accompanied those strikes made everyone dive for cover, but poor Duncan turned inside out with terror.

If we were in town and a storm came up, we tried to get home immediately because of Duncan. Our tie-out places had protection from the weather, but that didn't satisfy Duncan's idea of safety. Though no place inside the house served as a haven, either, he was insistent about getting in.

We had been in the new house we'd built on our farmland for only a few months when a storm came up. We hurried home from town, aware that Duncan, tied on the porch, would be frantic. By the time we got there, Duncan had gnawed one doorjamb almost completely away. It looked like a beaver had been at work on our new doors.

Often our storms were sound and fury, signifying nothing in the way of helpful moisture. So when the sky got quiet again, it was time to turn on the irrigation pump.

As soon as a storm passed, our quailing canine transformed into his assured, cheerful self. As I walked to the canal, Duncan pranced beside me, ears perked, muzzle sniffing the freshly washed air. He would try to get me to play by charging at me, growling, and dashing away. He suffered no posttraumatic symptoms.

When the pump began to hum, Duncan would turn and gaze toward the sprinklers. The body that had shivered with fear an hour before now quivered with excitement. He'd give me a happy grin over his shoulder and dash away.

A moment later, the black-and-white dancer would approach the first nozzle. As water sputtered from it, Duncan would pirouette once, twice, dancing after it. When water began to spray with more force, Duncan would do a series of *pas de chat*—small, graceful jumps. Soon, the pipes filled and the nozzles began to throw out streams of water. Then it was time for Duncan to execute *grand jetés*. He would launch his agile body heavenward, extend both front and back legs, toss his head toward the font, and sail, sail, sail. It was a celebration of health and life and movement and sunshine—and rain that came to the field in a miraculous way, unaccompanied by dreadful thunder and lightning.

NINE

Lala, a gray tabby, was in residence when Duncan arrived. She had come into our lives the year before as an insistent, stray kitten, following then three-year-old Mary and me on a downtown street. We tried to find her owner, but the people we asked said she'd been dumped. She came home with us.

When Duncan arrived as an enthusiastic pup, he brightened when he saw her, then galloped over to make her acquaintance. She swatted him on the nose and he jumped. Optimistic that she intended the swat as play, Duncan dropped onto his front legs and poked his wriggling rear end into the air. He barked, and she swatted him again. She actually had to swat him several times before he learned who clawfully reigned.

We came by a second cat soon after Duncan arrived. When we delivered Duncan to the vet to have him neutered, Mary and I met a beautiful orange cat, almost fully grown. She mewed at us from a cage in the lobby, and when Mary dangled her finger into the cage, the cat caught it with gentle paws, brought it to her face, and caressed it against her cheek. When I put my finger in the cage, the cat purred like a tractor. Mary and I were charmed.

"Is she always like this?" I asked the receptionist.

"Always. The Humane Association brought her in. She and her siblings were dumped in the foothills. They were starved, matted, and awful looking. They survived, so she probably is a good hunter."

We paid the adoption fee and took her home. It must have seemed a bad deal to Duncan that while he was enduring an operation, the number of cats at his home doubled.

In those days, Mary loved Sleeping Beauty—the book, the movie, the music. Mary named the new cat Aurora. The cat did resemble an orange dawn, arriving on every scene smiling and humming like a new morning.

She had a stubby tail, which can be characteristic of Manx cats, that she carried aloft except when she was hunting. I'd read that Manx would play like dogs, and we found that Aurora liked to chase a ball and bat it back to us.

For all her appearance of sweetness, she was a ruthless hunter. I liked to keep our animals on the slim side, but Aurora's body ranged from plump to blimp. In spring, when mice began to appear everywhere from under the melting snow, Aurora could hardly be persuaded to come in the house for ten minutes. She felt an urgency about catching and eating every emerging rodent. If Shane pleaded, "Rory, come sit on the couch with me," she would consent and even turn on her diesel purr. But she kept one watchful eye on the field beyond the glass doors so that if the grass fluttered, she could be off.

From my kitchen window, I often observed an orange stripe moving in the weeds. After a time Aurora would appear, strutting with a mouse or vole in her mouth. She did not dine right away; rather, she liked to make a victory march around the yard. Duncan and Lala would nose over to her, asking for a share in the spoils, but a low moan and stiffened fur would warn them off. By midsummer, Aurora looked like a pumpkin with feet.

Even with her large appetite, Aurora killed more than she could consume. Sometimes, she actually did share her bounty with the other animals. Still, bodies of dead mice lay everywhere. One night at a meeting of environmentalists and sheep producers, I heard a woman defend coyotes by saying, "Animals do not kill for recreation." I laughed aloud, thinking of the dead mice that littered our yard.

Aurora maintained a warm relationship with all the animals on the farm. (Maybe from her standpoint she lived in harmony with mice, too. They provided game; she kept their numbers in control. I suspect the mice did not feel the benefits of the relationship, though, and told tales around mouse campfires of a horrific orange beast.)

Aurora made a thorough round of pens every day, visiting horses, sheep, and, later on, goats and pigs. If lambs or piglets were racing in play, Aurora sat on the fence, purring and watching with approval, reaching her paw out to bat them as they tore past. Our children weren't permitted to enter the ram pen because rams can be territorial and dangerous, but Aurora liked to rub herself against their legs and faces, and they never lowered their heads to butt.

When we started raising chickens, Aurora added calling on their pen to her tour; when Shane raised 4-H ducks, she befriended them as well. We had three beehives on the ridge behind the house and sometimes Aurora took a stroll to see them. As bees hummed in and out of the hive, Aurora would stand on hind legs and judiciously peer inside, the sound of her purr blending with the buzz from the bees.

Her most dramatic instance of breaking down interspecies barriers came when we agreed to let friends keep their llamas at our place.

The day the llamas arrived, every normally calm animal on the place went berserk. Duncan barked in a high-pitched yip I'd never heard before. The horses tore around their corral, terror on their faces. The ewes hightailed it to the farthest corner of the pasture and went into a huddle. Neighbors came onto their porches to see what the dust and commotion were about.

The llamas stood in the middle of a backyard pen, eyes wide, limbs stiff.

Aurora watched all this from her perch on the fence. Then she hopped down and strolled into the midst of the new arrivals.

Llamas have natural curiosity, and the biggest one, a male, approached Aurora, extending his long neck and dropping his head. He huffed his exotic breath on her, moved his lips over her fur, and brought an eye around to stare. His two llama friends came over and joined in. Aurora sat perfectly still as the three gave her a complete going over, but I noticed her patient expression starting to fade.

Suddenly, Aurora whirled and slashed the biggest llama on the nose. He jumped a couple of feet in the air and so did his startled friends. Then the cat turned, gazed at the resident animals peering over the fence, and began to wash her face. The hierarchy had been established. She added calling on llamas to her daily rounds.

Aurora's favorites were the horses. While it was amazing enough to see her climb onto Duncan when he was lying down, painstakingly arrange herself, and snuggle down for a nap, it was more incredible to see her do the same thing atop the horses.

Aurora would walk the top pole of the horse corral until she found herself beside a resting horse. Then she would hop onto its back, stretch, work her claws, circle, and lie down for a nap. Most often the horse was Lucy, Shane's bay mare, who would cock an ear and look questioningly over her shoulder. But Lucy would remain still as long as Aurora was napping.

One day when I was riding in the corral, Aurora paced back and forth on the corral, mewing. I wasn't sure what she was trying to convey, but I rode over, plucked her off the fence and placed her in front of me in the saddle. As the horse swayed off, Aurora gave her loudest diesel purr. After that, if any of us noticed Aurora pacing the fence, we picked her up and took her for a ride. Her feline body conformed to the swell in the saddle, and she enjoyed trotting even more than walking.

Our farrier at the time was on the jumpy side. When trimming hooves or shoeing, he kept a wary eye, even with a sleepy, gentle horse. He was quick to discipline—too quick, I thought—and sometimes he riled an otherwise calm horse. One day when he was working on Rainbow, Matt's buckskin, I looked out the window and saw Aurora pacing the fence.

"No, kitty," I muttered, but it was too late. She took a leap onto Rainbow's back.

The farrier, holding one of Rainbow's back legs between his legs, was facing away, but he felt something when the cat landed. He turned to have a look. His eyes widened.

Just then, I reached the corral.

"This horse gonna blow up?" He looked ready to flee.

"No. She likes the cat."

Aurora rolled, writhing with pleasure, then dug her claws into Rainbow's neck and began to sharpen them. The farrier, holding the horse's leg, froze. I grabbed Aurora and took her in the house.

At chore time, Aurora liked to trot beside the person feeding. In wild winds, with snow swirling, I would pick her up and tuck her inside my insulated coveralls. But she would have none of it; she would squirm free and take her customary place, running along beside me. I could hear her purring. It's true the walk for her wasn't as arduous as for me, since I had to trudge through drifts while Aurora padded atop the snow. Still, raw temperatures and stinging wind must have penetrated to her bones. But tail in the air like a pendant, she trotted beside me until the last flake of hay had been distributed. Duncan tried to squeeze between her and me, but often, Aurora edged him out.

Duncan, while learning to share the family's attention with two cats, passed out of puppyhood. Though easy to train, Duncan had done his share of destroying property, and in exuberant moments, he had torn around like a lunatic.

But when he turned a year old, it was like he'd read the calendar and decided to put away childish behavior. The destruction came to an abrupt stop. His intense side, which always had been a part of his nature, now dominated. He devoted his energy to doing chores with his humans, making certain the sheep were where they needed to be, and staying close enough to family members so that if either cat came near, he could offer a ready alternative.

He embodied everything we could possibly want in a dog, and I believe, with his confidence and dignity, he saw it that way, too. So it must have been disappointing for him when we brought home a superfluous second dog.

TEN

We bought a Great Pyrenees pup because stray dogs were killing sheep all over the county.

Every year at the local Wool Growers' Banquet, two topics of conversation dominated: the price being paid for lamb and wool, and marauding dogs. Lamb consumption in America had shrunk and imported lamb from New Zealand and Australia had hurt domestic producers. A worldwide glut meant wool prices had declined. Even so, terms for contracts could vary and sometimes optimism crept into discussions about the market. But reports about predator dogs caused alarm year after year.

County leash laws forbid dogs to run free. The law favored livestock raisers, and if a stray were picked up for chasing livestock, it couldn't be adopted. If a licensed dog were caught harming livestock, the owner was held liable for losses. But in a county so large it encompassed mountain ranges and valleys on one side and desert on the other, enforcement proved impossible.

Singly, in pairs or in packs, dogs skulked onto sheep farms at night. Dogs would sometimes attack in the daytime, too, and a working couple might come home to a bloody mess. Certain dog breeds had terrible reputations and sheep raisers hated to spot them hanging around the neighborhood—Labradors, retrievers, German shepherds, and huskies. The yellow Labrador who made a model family pet could cause a scene in a livestock pen that would sicken a war veteran. As more people moved out from town to the country, dog problems increased. People buying acreages had a notion that at last their dog could run free.

Our neighbors the Kirbys had microphones in their barn hooked up to speakers in their bedroom so if they heard a commotion in the night, Elwood could get to the barn quickly. When a black Labrador belonging to another neighbor began showing up at the Kirby place, I called the dog's owner to warn her.

"It's dangerous for your dog to be running the neighborhood. Elwood Kirby shoots dogs that get in his sheep."

"He can't do that!"

"He can," I said. "It's the law."

"Do you shoot dogs?"

"We don't have guns, but I call the pound." When I'd first had sheep, I'd once returned a neighbor's dog to its owners after it inflicted terrible injuries to a wonderful old ewe named Critter. I'd slept in the barn with her the night of the attack because she was so traumatized, and treated her wounds morning and night for two weeks after.

One morning I inspected Critter's rear end and saw that the gaping wounds over her hips had begun to close. "You're going to make it," I told her.

That afternoon I came home and found the same dog atop Critter, gnawing on her flanks. I jumped out of the car, screaming, and the dog fled. When I went back to the veterinarian to buy more medicine he told me, "You don't understand the rule. When a dog gets into your sheep, you plant the dog."

Now I told my friend, "Keep your dog home or you might lose him."

She said they'd been chaining him, but he was an intact male and clever about escaping.

A few nights later, Elwood awakened to a ruckus, rushed to the sheep pen, and found the black Lab chasing pregnant ewes. Blood and wool dripped from the dog's mouth. Elwood shot it dead.

The dog's owners believed their pet had only meant to be playful. In their grief, they suspected there was more to it. They were non-Mormon in a mostly Mormon neighborhood. Not a Mormon, either,

I assured them religion had nothing to do with it. "In the dark," I said, "Elwood couldn't tell the dog was Baptist."

Before long, tragedy struck the Kirbys again. A pair of golden retrievers got into their sheep pen and wreaked havoc. Some ewes died in the attack, some didn't die until weeks later. The dogs' owners settled a claim for losses, but money hardly compensated the Kirbys for their disappointment. They had cultivated desirable genes over the years, and some of their best ewes had perished.

We had a high-voltage, dog-proof fence, but the fence had to be well maintained to work properly. Weeds could cause the fence to short out. A motivated dog could dig under it. Besides that, a dog could enter through our horse corral to reach our lambing shed.

I read up on llamas, sometimes used as flock guardians. They were expensive and studies had shown them to be ineffective once a predator got used to the llama's curiosity. Donkeys had been successful as guardians but could be dangerous to family dogs as well as invading ones. We couldn't put Duncan in jeopardy.

The U.S. Sheep Experiment Station was conducting research on dogs historically used to guard flocks in Europe. The station had imported komondors, Akbashs, Anatolian shepherds, Maremmas, and Great Pyrenees. The scientists raised the puppies with young lambs and the puppies bonded with them. When the dogs grew up, they would protect the flock from danger. A herding dog like Duncan could alert us to intruders but wouldn't be as effective in running them off as a large dog bred for guarding.

A Great Pyrenees looked most suitable for us because of its gentle temperament. We had young children at our house regularly and couldn't have a dog that would be aggressive with people.

A sheep station researcher told me, "If you buy a puppy, you must not handle it. You don't want it to bond with you; you want it to bond with sheep."

"We're supposed to have a cuddly puppy on the place and not touch it? We have three children who love animals."

"If you know you can't resist handling a puppy . . ."

"We can't."

". . . then resolve to handle it only thirty minutes a day."

I located a litter of pups being sold by a sheep rancher. When George and I got out of our car at the ranch, a giant white dog ran to greet us. Anna, mother of the pups, jumped up and put her paws on my shoulders. The rancher hastened to scold her. "We try not to handle her," he said.

The rancher grazed sheep on high desert and said that before getting Anna and his other guardians, predation from coyotes had threatened to close him down. The dogs had made it possible for him to continue in business. The previous season, Anna had fought a cougar to protect her flock. (Years later, we heard Anna had died in a fight with a bear.)

At that moment, Anna was gazing fondly at a little boy who was stroking her head. "Don't pet her, son," the rancher said.

The pups, snowballs with gray eye masks, were cuter than I'd imagined. George and I watched the pups at play and one, the largest and a female, seemed to be dominant. Dominance seemed like a desirable trait for a guardian. We said we'd be back for her in two weeks.

The day we came back, the rancher wasn't home. The children were snuggling pups when we arrived. Their mother said, "Don't handle them, kids," while she herself stroked Anna. I relaxed a bit about the ban on handling a guard dog. Anna had retained her bravery and protectiveness despite the attentions of a large, dog-loving family.

We named our puppy Gracie. Sheep-raising friends and town-dwelling Ronna dropped by to have a look at her. Gracie had a flat nose, which would lengthen with age, an innocent stare, which she would never lose, and huge feet, which would grow bigger.

We might not have kept our vow to have her in the house for short, prescribed periods, except that she didn't much like the house. After twenty minutes, she would whimper and go to the door. Perhaps with her thick coat she got too hot inside the house. Anyway, she wanted to get back to her sheep. We kept her in a pen with bum lambs, with whom she played and slept. When she wandered over to visit ewes and their babies, the ewes lowered their heads and drove her away. But as she grew up, the ewes came to regard her as one of them, and she slept in their midst.

Her protectiveness showed itself almost at once. She developed a habit of putting herself between a visitor and me, or a visitor and Mary. She didn't have the same protective response toward the boys and George, though I believe if the occasion had called for it, she would have protected any of us.

I liked to roughhouse with my sons, but we instinctively knew not to do this when Gracie was around. She might have felt compelled to defend me. When delivery people brought packages to the house or the meter reader arrived, she positioned herself between them and me, watching with a placid but attentive expression. I never saw anyone who didn't understand what the look meant.

She was only a few months old when we sent our early lambs to market. As George and the boys were sorting and loading lambs, I heard a scratching at the back door. I opened it and found Gracie.

"What's wrong?" I asked, holding the door open for her. She didn't want to come in. She dashed down the porch stairs, turned around, and waited for me. I followed.

In the paddock, Gracie circled the truck worriedly. She wanted me to know that lambs—not her bum lamb friends but older ones—had been put in the trailer. I hardly knew what to tell her. Parting with lambs would be a fact of her life. We sold most of our ewe lambs for breeding stock, but we sold wethers, the castrated males, for meat. In both cases, the lambs left our care.

I sat down on the porch steps and petted her. "I've never gotten used to it myself," I said.

Gracie had the characteristics of an alpha dog—she never licked the face of any human or dog or lay on her back in submission. But Aurora the cat was too much for her. The orange cat loved to taunt the big dog. Aurora would show up with a mouse in her mouth, parading across Gracie's path. If Gracie ignored her, Aurora would come close and stroke herself against the dog's chest, mouse dangling within snatching distance of the dog's mouth. Gracie's muzzle would begin to edge toward the mouse. Aurora would swell up and give a threatening moan, causing Gracie to recoil. No matter how often Aurora pulled this trick, the good-hearted, trusting Gracie always got suckered.

Gracie did acknowledge Duncan's seniority. This put her in a bit of a dilemma. She didn't think she should run him off when he got near her sheep, but at the same time, she wasn't going to stand still while any dog messed with her flock. She handled this with tact and creativity. When Duncan showed up to move sheep, she ran at him, her face cheerful, and tried to lure him into a game. Duncan, of course, would have none of it and tried to duck around her. But she was a sizable obstacle. Gracie eventually got used to Duncan's role at feeding time, but any other time when we were sorting or moving sheep, Gracie had to be taken in the house so Duncan could do his job.

I gazed out my kitchen window. Beside the barn, wild strawberries bloomed with dainty white flowers. Ewes resting in the pasture chewed their cud while their lambs popcorned, springing into the air with all four feet off the ground at once. One bunch of lambs tore up a hillside of manure in a frantic game of tag. Gracie napped beneath the shade of a sagebrush.

It was Shane's first summer raising pigs, and in the pen he'd built, piglets raced and squealed. Aurora was asleep atop Lucy, Shane's mare. Lala, perched on a corral pole, reached down to bat at Duncan's tail.

Duncan noticed the lambs gamboling and sat up. Sheep moving without his direction troubled him.

"It's okay," I said out the window to him. "They can play."

He lay back down.

It was the Peaceable Kingdom. We had two exceptional dogs, two foolishly affectionate cats, calm horses, and terrific ewes. To have this collection of wonderful animals all at one time seemed like phenomenal fortune.

The Peaceable Kingdom. That's what our farm resembled.

I reached for a Kleenex and blew my nose. I'd picked up another cold.

Summer

·····················

ELEVEN

A chilly June rain fell and a sharp wind blew out of the north. Despite that, when I pulled up at a farm north of town, I had to park a long way from the barn. Dozens of vehicles, mostly pickup trucks, crowded the yard.

The dog trainer had attracted a good turnout. Flyers posted at local feed stores had advertised that during the morning session, the trainer would demonstrate his herd dogs. After lunch, the trainer would work with spectators' dogs. A day off with Duncan had sounded like a great break.

The strong turnout despite nasty weather surprised me, but it shouldn't have. Ranchers took their dogs and the work they performed seriously. Years before, when I'd written *Alone on the Mountain*, about the lives of western sheepherders, I'd hung around the Idaho mountains during one halcyon spring and summer with sheep outfits. The lifestyle of herders had changed little since ancient times. The herder lived in a simple, portable sheep camp when he moved the flock to summer pastures in the mountains, and dogs and horses helped him carry out his tasks. I'd heard dozens of fascinating stories about stock dogs, but two in particular had made an impression on me.

One told of a herder who was tending sheep atop a southeastern Idaho mountain when a storm hit. Lightning killed the herder, a dog, several sheep, and started a forest fire. The surviving Border collie ran through fiery terrain rounding up the scattered flock and moved them off the mountain. The dog kept the sheep bunched in a meadow. When the rancher located them a couple of days later, he found the dog exhausted, hungry, thirsty, and ill from burns and smoke inhalation. Its feet were raw and bleeding from running itself ragged, but it had kept the sheep together.

Another story involved a herder who stole a dog from a neighboring herder. The dog's rightful owner set out to find his dog. When he did, an argument erupted, and the dog's owner shot and killed the other man.

When the case came before a judge, the judge imposed a minimum sentence on the man who had killed the thief. I remarked to the sheepman who told me the story that I would have expected a western judge to be more stern. With complete sincerity the sheepman said, "The judge understood that a man can't do his job without a good dog."

Around the corral that Saturday, men and women who hoped to make their good dogs better huddled, hands in pockets, hats pulled down. The demonstrations did not disappoint. The dogs pushed sheep through gates and into enclosures. Pups herded ducks for practice, scattering squawking birds everywhere. The trainer talked a bit about his methods, but mostly he showed how to do it.

His dogs rested in kennels when they weren't working. The trainer said not to make pets of working dogs. I glanced down at Duncan, who, coincidentally, was looking up at me. "No, that doesn't apply to you," I said.

Some experts believed stock dogs should be in crates when not working, so the dogs wouldn't expend their energy in playing. Their excitement would be reserved for working. And because of their intelligence, Border collies left on their own could get into mischief. But Duncan never lacked enthusiasm for herding sheep, and when he wasn't working, he stayed occupied with his role as companion dog.

After lunch, the trainer took dogs from the crowd and worked with them. When it was Duncan's turn, I was eager to see what the trainer would think of him.

He asked Duncan to do a variety of maneuvers. I couldn't tell how my dog was doing because everything in the corral happened fast and the trainer spoke so softly I couldn't hear what he said. When he returned Duncan to me the man said, "If you don't know what you're doing, it's best to let the dog teach you. This dog knows what to do, but someone has made him inhibited."

I felt embarrassed the trainer could tell Duncan knew more than his handlers, but a woman standing next to me felt worse. She drew disapproving looks from onlookers because her dog barked incessantly. Compared to the poised dogs who sat beside their owners watching the action in the corral, the noisy dog seemed like it must be another breed altogether, though it obviously was a Border collie.

The woman told me, "I know she's getting on everyone's nerves. But we live in town and she wants to work so badly, I thought it'd be nice for her to be around livestock. Now I see this wasn't a good idea."

Just then the dog yowled because she caught her head in the fence while trying to nip a sheep running past.

The trainer invited the dog into the corral. The dog boiled into the midst of the sheep, scattered them helter-skelter, and raced in circles. She was too high to listen to the trainer, who was urging her to calm down.

The trainer observed, "This is why it isn't good to have these dogs in town. They need to work."

Driving home, I thought about the woman, her dog, and the trainer's words. I had written a young adult novel the year before about a boy and his two draft horses. Now another idea came to me. What if a kid who lived in town fell head-over-teacups for a Border collie? What problems would be caused by the dog's great desire to work?

During the next weeks I sketched out a plot, experimented with characters, read more on stock dogs, and watched my own dog closely. I came up with an idea that Terry, the protagonist, would teach Duffy, his Border collie, tricks to occupy the dog's mind. And with a dog act, Terry could help out his impoverished family.

I checked out a library book on dog tricks and went to work. The book said a dog who loves to eat is easy to train, and recommended rewarding the dog with hot dogs. I picked up a package on my next trip to town.

Duncan knew basic obedience commands—sit, stay, heel, and come, so I skipped past them. The first trick I undertook was "walk."

The dog had to "sit" first. Then the trainer suspended a piece of hot dog above the dog. This inspired the dog to stand. The trainer rewarded the dog with the bite of hot dog. It might take several training sessions for the dog to get used to standing on his hind legs; after that, the trainer could proceed to "walk."

To teach "walk," the trainer, holding the treat above the dog's head, backed up. Ideally, the dog would follow the food. But the book warned many dogs would sit down rather than move forward on their hind legs.

"Ready to try this, Duncan?"

Duncan, who loved food, could smell the hot dog. He looked eager.

"Duncan, *up*." I held the hot dog above his head. He stood on his hind legs and balanced, nose upward. He'd had practice with this position because he often assumed it to get guests to notice him.

"Sit," I said. He sat and I gave him the hot dog.

"Up," I said. He stood on his hind legs again. The book said to allow the dog to get comfortable with standing before moving on. Duncan looked comfortable.

"Walk." I backed up, holding the piece of hot dog. Duncan came forward on his hind legs.

"Good dog!" I gave him the treat and ruffled his hair.

I glanced at the book. "Walk" would take a week to teach, it said, but I thought Duncan had it down.

I turned the page to "Sitting on a Stool." The book's author thought this an important trick from the showmanship angle. When the trainer brought the dog into the room, made him sit on a stool, summoned the dog for a trick, then sent him back to the stool, it gave a professional look to the performance.

I looked around in the barn and found a step stool I'd bought for

Mary when she was little. I hosed off the dust and Duncan and I went to the front yard.

"Dunc, this is 'place.' 'Place.'" I tapped it. "Here. Get up on it." He did. "Now, sit." He did. I held my hand in front of his face. "Stay." I walked away. Looking uneasy, Duncan stayed. He'd never liked that command.

"Duncan, come." He dashed over to me. I walked him back to the stool. "Place," I said. He hopped onto it. "Sit." He did.

I called him to me again. Then I wondered if I could send him back to the stool on his own, or if it was too soon to try that. During times when Duncan and I worked sheep, I used an arm signal that meant, "Go out." Now I waved my arm in the "Go out" motion and said, "Go to place." He flew to the stool, jumped onto it, and sat down.

From the standpoint of teaching a dog tricks, everything was going great. But as a research exercise aimed at showing me the frustrations of training a dog to perform, it fell short.

The book's author recommended keeping sessions short. I decided we'd done enough. The next day I'd try something complicated. "Jumping Through a Hoop."

I found an old rake handle for the next day's session. The first step was to get the dog to jump over a stick. The handler held the stick low at first, and held a hot dog piece on the other side to tempt the dog to jump over.

Duncan knew "over" already because I used that word to invite him into the sheep pen. He could sail over a tall fence. So I skipped the low height and even the hot dog at first. I held the handle at thigh height and said, "Over." Duncan leaped over.

"Good dog." I invited him to jump back the other way.

Once the dog understood "over," the handler was to hold out his arm instead of the stick. When the handler got the dog jumping over his arm, he could use his other arm to form a circle.

I'd known the first steps would go fast. But I thought Duncan might balk at jumping through my arms-turned-hoop. He did look puzzled when I added my other arm, and when I said, "Over" he looked around for the handle. After a minute, it clicked with him and he jumped through my arms.

We'd accomplished way more than I'd expected. I didn't want to push Duncan, even though he seemed to be having a good time.

If Duffy in the book was smart like Duncan, my character Terry wouldn't need patience to put together a dog act. So I put Terry under a time crunch, giving him only nine days to put together a routine for a kid's birthday party.

The training book went back to the library. I showed Duncan's tricks to the family and then forgot about them. But every Saturday morning, Duncan "walked" to get a pancake or two.

Writing the book didn't go as smoothly as teaching tricks to Duncan. I got lost, changed direction, dropped characters, simplified the plot, and rewrote the ending a dozen times.

I sent the draft manuscript to my dog trainer friend Lezlie to get her feedback. She called me as soon as she finished it.

"It's not believable that Duffy could learn that act in nine days. He couldn't perfect a trick a day."

"I tried some of the tricks with Duncan. He learned them in a day."

"No."

"Yes."

She sighed. "Border collies."

My editor called to say she liked the book, and suggested the title Some Fine Dog. The book came out a year later and the Junior Library Guild picked it up as a selection. Duncan started getting letters. A reference book on children's authors had run a picture of Duncan and me and mentioned I was receptive to mail. Kids sent letters to both of us, but Duncan got the most effusive ones.

I'd gotten used to people falling for Duncan in person. I hadn't foreseen that his picture would attract people, too. And I'd never anticipated there would be days when the mail consisted of a few pieces for the family—mostly bills and advertising—and several personal letters for Duncan.

Letters I received sometimes had the laborious feel of a class writing assignment. The kids made canned comments and urged me to write back. I suspected that receiving a letter back helped the student's grade.

Other letters reflected genuine involvement with the book. Young readers asked, "What happened to Terry after the book ended?" or reported, "I cried for Terry when . . ." Some letters came from children who were writing to a distant and therefore safe person, and confided information they might not have told to neighbors or teachers.

But all the letters to Duncan brimmed with sincerity. The letters might be bouncy or wistful, funny or solemn, but they were full of love.

> *Dear Duncan,*
>   *I live in Texas. Me and my parents work in the fields. I don't have a dog because we move too much. I know a dog named Iggy and I play with her sometimes.*
>   *I am like Terry. I think about what I will do when I grow up, like not move so much and have a horse and a dog, and go where it is not so hot. Do you like working with sheep?*
>   *I love you,*
>   *Gilberto*

Some kids told Duncan about their own dogs—tricks they could do, what they liked to eat, what annoying traits they had.

When I wrote back, I didn't pretend to be Duncan. I said, "I read Duncan your letter and he seemed very interested." Then I would talk about Duncan's life on the farm and thank the child for writing.

Another phenomenon centering on Duncan began about the same time. Guests who'd stayed at our house often wrote their thank-you notes to Duncan, telling him how much they'd enjoyed meeting him. Or if the letters didn't come directly to Duncan, friends or relatives mentioned I should give Duncan their warm regards.

A friend I met through a writer's organization greatly admired Duncan. Tom lived in Salt Lake City and sent a letter addressed to "Mr. Duncan Sherlock," written in Dog.

Dear Duncan,
Woof! A-ooooo-ooo-a-oo. Woof! Whine? Sniff, grrr-woof!

. . . and so on.

When I read the letter to Duncan, he had a puzzling reaction. He went to the door, moaned, and wanted out. I wondered if my friend, not fully understanding Dog, had said something troubling. He may have intended to say, "How's it going?" but like others who have stumbled using a foreign language (President John Kennedy, who told Berliners he was a doughnut), Tom might have said "A wolf pack will arrive at 4 P.M." Or "The UPS man is a steak sandwich on a hoagie roll."

I wrote Tom back and told him of Duncan's response, and my theory that he may have conveyed something he didn't intend. Tom thought the problem was mine.

"Though you tried your best," he wrote, "you may have failed to convey precise collie nuances, and if you'd said, 'Woof' in the way I intended, Duncan wouldn't have been upset."

Duncan was the object of so much correspondence, I decided he should author the annual Christmas letter. Because the letter was from a canine viewpoint, it contained lots of news about the animals who shared his life.

The letter brought warm responses. From a serious clergyman came a letter thanking Duncan for his thoughtfulness and recalling the pleasant moments he'd spent in Duncan's company. A former boss of mine wrote and asked if he and his wife could come for a visit so they could meet the remarkable writer of the Christmas letter. My sister, Bobbette, who wrote impeccable letters, usually serious in tone, wrote to Duncan that the Christmas letter this year "seemed more personal. I know that's because it came from your heart, Duncan."

TWELVE

....

Duncan was ever ready to make up a new game and initiate fun. He wore a perpetual doggy grin, but he had a puritanical side. Duncan would not permit dancing.

"R-E-S-P-E-C-T!" *The voice of Aretha Franklin blared on the stereo.* I'd put on rock music to energize myself for cleaning. Now I ran the dust rag over the piano, jerking my shoulders and flicking my hips.

Mary swiveled over to join me. Rolling her shoulders, she lifted a decorative pot off the piano and handed it to me to dust.

Matt, sprawled on the sofa reading a book, got up and left. He disliked the music, but my hopelessly behind-the-times moves probably distressed him, too. Shane was outside helping George.

I turned up the music and boogied over to plug in the vacuum. Mary threw back her head, snapped her upper body forward, and pushed her hands away from her body.

I sang, "All I'm askin' (oo) is for a little respect when you come home (just a little bit)."

The kitchen door opened and a moment later Duncan burst into the living room. He ran straight at me, jumped on my thigh, and barked.

"No, Duncan." I danced back to the vacuum.

"WOOF!" Duncan jumped onto my legs again.

"No!" I repeated.

He dashed over to Mary, who was raking her hand through her hair in a suggestive way I might have disapproved of had it not been cleaning day.

Duncan jumped on her leg and threw her off balance.

She faltered but caught herself. "Bad dog!" she scolded.

Shane, who'd come in with Duncan, hollered, "Whose music is this!"

I resumed wiggling to the rhythm, but Duncan came back and faced me. "WOOF!" he said angrily.

"Just a minute." I turned down the music. "Duncan, come."

He walked through the kitchen with me, and I opened the back door. "Outside."

He obeyed, but threw a worried look over his shoulder.

I turned up the music and turned the vacuum on, and pushed it across the living room with syncopated motions. "R-E-S-P-E-C-T!" I belted.

Duncan made an exception for ballet. Mary loved an audience and often performed after-dinner recitals for us. Sometimes she planned them down to small details, including costuming and choosing music, and rehearsed for a week. Sometimes the recitals were spontaneous; Mary put on the music and improvised. All the performances were laden with drama. Mary assumed a solemn face, pulled her arms close to her, then threw them out, thrust forward her chest, and skittered across the room. Grand jetés, like Duncan himself performed outside when he danced with sprinklers, did not trouble him, even though Mary executed them in the cramped kitchen.

That led me at first to think it was rock music he objected to. But sometimes a gentle waltz came on the radio, and if George and I stood up, assumed a dance posture and began swirling around the kitchen, Duncan appeared from nowhere and protested with a WOOF! He tried to grab the legs of our jeans with his teeth to prevent us from moving.

Normally, he wanted to please us, but we couldn't make him stop harassing us about dancing. Always, we had to put him outside. He permitted ballet, but Duncan believed other dancing, whether ballroom or rock, had to be stopped.

THIRTEEN

....

"Go get 'er, Duncan!" I yelled. Duncan streaked after a recalcitrant ewe.

George, Duncan, and I had successfully penned all the sheep, but before I got the gate tied, a ewe had forced her way out and run off to the field.

"Why didn't you stop her!" George complained.

"She just—" I stopped. "I'm sorry."

I saw that sheep were unpredictable, and sometimes they just escaped, but deep down, I suspected the fault had been mine. That doubt in me felt ancient. Maybe, centuries before at the dawn of agriculture, some inattentive woman had let a primitive tool fall on her husband's bare foot, and I still carried the guilt.

Duncan rounded up the obstinate ewe and ran her into the pen. I quickly tied the gate with twine.

On a shelf in the barn, we'd lined up small bread pans that held our supplies—vaccine, cotton balls, alcohol, and syringes. George had bottles of vaccine in his shirt pocket.

We followed a method. George would catch a ewe, pull her out of the pen, and I would give her a shot. Mary would join us to act as bookkeeper, recording the ear tag numbers of which ewes had received shots. If any ewe escaped before getting a shot, we'd have a record of the vaccinated ones.

In a few minutes, we were under way, and after an hour, we had made good progress. But then we encountered a ewe who wanted to fight. As George pulled the animal from the pen, she jumped into the air. George, holding her around the neck, got thrown off balance. He and the ewe went down. I still had a syringe in my hand. I grabbed for the ewe and accidentally stuck George in the hand with the needle.

"Ouch!" he hollered.

"Oh! I'm sorry."

Duncan dashed to George, who was shaking his hand and cussing, then ran to me. He sat down and gazed up at me with a worried expression. Unlike Gracie, who put herself between me and others, when Duncan felt tension between George and me he tried to diffuse it by being genial. If that didn't work, he sat down and leaned against my leg. If he intended to be reassuring, it worked.

I wanted to joke that George wouldn't have to worry about getting white muscle disease now. But the ewe was still struggling, so I tossed the syringe onto the shelf and grabbed hold of her.

"Got 'er?" George asked.

"Yeah." I wrapped my arms around her.

George got to his feet and dusted off his pants. But the ewe got a second wind and lunged forward. I lost my grip. The ewe thundered out of the barn, with Duncan giving chase.

"You let 'er go!"

"She lurched and I—" I got a familiar, defeated feeling. "Sorry."

George said, "Now we'll have to pen all the sheep when we're done and check all their ear tags. Instead of being done an hour from now, it will take three." I didn't fully hear him; I had recriminations going on in my own head.

"I'm going to go in and make lunch." I dragged to the house.

While I was making sandwiches, the phone rang. It was the president of a local writer's group, inviting me to speak at their meeting the following Saturday.

"I'd love to!" I'd get to visit with people I hadn't seen for a while. I would hear about interesting writing projects. And I wouldn't be home the next weekend to help George with the next phase of vaccinating.

"Only one scoop? Maybe you should have two." Dave from my writer's group pointed at the glass case and tubs of ice cream. "They have so many to choose from."

"I always get one scoop of chocolate mint chip." Our writer's group had wrapped up early, and Dave and I had walked to a nearby ice cream shop.

"How many flavors have you tried?" he asked.

"A few. But I've settled on a favorite."

"You've given up adventure?"

We were only talking ice cream, but suddenly I felt worn out.

"Adventure and my present life don't go together."

Dave lifted an eyebrow. "Say more."

"I have a lot of responsibility." I forced back my shoulders and gave the clerk a smile and my cone order.

Dave ordered rocky road and butter pecan. "Are your responsibilities of your own choosing?"

Dave spent a lot of time thinking about how to live his life well and I liked hearing his ideas, but I didn't take him too seriously. He was single, lived in an apartment, had no animals, and no children. When Dave and I talked about responsibility, we were calling to each other across a chasm.

"Did I choose to be married? Have children? Be a partner in a sheep business? Yeah. I chose all of it."

"How seriously do you take your responsibility to yourself?"

"I take care of myself, if that's what you mean. I exercise and eat right."

"If your sheep or your husband or the kids needed something, but you needed something, too, like a nap, would you take the nap?"

Wow, did Dave and I have different lives. A nap, even as a concept, never entered my mind.

"If you *needed* the nap . . ." Dave prodded.

"Like, if I were sick?"

"No. Like if you were tired."

I didn't answer. I leaned against the ice cream case, tired enough for a nap that very minute.

We sat at a table with wrought iron chairs and started to eat our cones. Dave, I noticed, was watching me.

"Who do you think is responsible for your life?"

"Me, of course." I knew the correct answer to give. But if I'd been truthful I would have answered differently. George was responsible for my life, and I for his. That was the nature of partnership, wasn't it?

"If you look around," Dave said, "you see that people think it's up to someone else—their spouse or employer or society—to give them what they need." He shrugged. "You can't blame them."

"No?"

"It's seductive, making someone else responsible. And deep down, a person may know if he starts taking responsibility for himself, a lot can change."

"What do you mean?"

"Sometimes, a person loses everything."

"I don't follow."

"A person attracts people into his life that buy into his fiction—that he's not responsible. They may not believe themselves responsible, either. So when a person starts taking responsibility for himself, he puts a lot at risk."

A feeling like electricity had started to tingle my scalp.

"People are loath to look at the ways they don't take responsibility," Dave said.

"Because they fear where it might lead."

"Exactly."

I stared out the window at an apple tree. Its blossoms had fallen and small apples had set on. Purple geraniums encircled the base of the tree.

"Gotta go." I stood up.

"Before you finish your cone?"

"Oh. No." I sat back down. "I'll finish my cone." That was weird. Forgetting I had an ice cream cone in my hand.

Duncan was waiting for me when I got back to my car. I reached through the open window and stroked his head. His tongue flicked out and gave my hand a fond kiss.

Driving home, I thought about the conversation with Dave. Philosophizing made for interesting conversation, but by the time I reached my own driveway, I intended to put abstraction behind me.

FOURTEEN

The concierge stared across the lobby of Salt Lake City's DoubleTree hotel, directly at me.

"Eyes forward," I mumbled to Matt and Shane, who were fourteen, and Mary, who was seven. They swiveled their heads, trying to see what they weren't supposed to look at. Only Duncan, walking close to my heel, looked straight ahead at the elevator, our destination.

During the three days we'd stayed at the hotel, I'd been on edge every time I walked through the lobby with Duncan. But I'd strolled through at all times of day and night and no hotel employee had said a word. Maybe they hadn't noticed Duncan because he walked in and out of the hotel pressed close to my leg. Maybe hotel employees had decided he was an assistance dog who aided me with a hidden disability.

If Duncan got kicked out, he could stay at the Salt Palace with the sheep George and I had brought to the National Ram Sale. That wasn't uncommon; many a herd dog slept tied to its family's sheep pens. But Border collies sometimes were stolen, and Duncan was a handsome dog. He could have slept in the locked cab of our pickup, too, but he liked being with the family and caused no trouble.

The concierge's stare scalded me. I refused to acknowledge his glare and continued toward the elevator. "Don't look," I ordered again in a low voice.

"Don't look where?" the kids asked, rubbernecking.

"That man over there is gawking," Mary said. She had been taught not to gawk.

Elsewhere in the lobby, men and women in business attire milled. Two men sitting in overstuffed chairs wore Stetsons and string ties, and one I recognized as the sheep auctioneer. Still, the atmosphere fairly shouted, "No dogs!"

Suddenly the concierge, in a forbidding dark suit, face fixed in a scowl, stepped into my path.

"Madame," he said, with a faint foreign accent. "Iss that a dog?"

I looked at Duncan, then looked the man in the eye.

"No." I smiled. "That's *Duncan*."

The concierge looked annoyed. "We do not—"

Duncan sat down daintily and gazed up at the man. His black ears stood at attention and his insistent brown eyes watched the concierge's face. He spent much time in dusty corrals and received few proper brushings; yet, his black-and-white coat glistened with natural good health.

"We do not—"

Duncan got up, moved a step forward, and sat down again. He cocked his head, peering intensely at the man, and his lips fell back in a modest canine smile.

"Dogs aren't—"

Duncan's head pushed forward a bit. The blaze that ran down his muzzle and melted into a wide, white ruff came level with the man's hand. Duncan deliberated. Then a red tongue came out and gave the hand the merest genteel lick. Duncan let his head fall back again so he could ogle the man, and his tail gave a satisfied wag.

"We don't—" The man's brows knotted, then unknotted.

Duncan, already fifty pounds of concentrated attention, became more absorbed in the concierge. His look said, "What you are going to say must be really wonderful, because you, sir, are obviously wonderful."

If Duncan unwittingly had become part of a staring contest, he now emerged as the winner. The man glanced at the chandeliers and coughed. Without saying anything, he stepped out of our path. The kids and I hurried to the elevator. Duncan looked back affectionately at his new friend.

The next morning I took Duncan out for an early walk. When the elevator opened to the lobby, I found myself nose to nose with a plump bellhop. The pudgy guy looked down at Duncan.

"Hey! We don't allow dogs," he said.

I started to apologize. Then I noticed the concierge watching us from across the lobby. Duncan, too, saw him and gave a happy look of recognition and waved his tail.

The bellhop called to the concierge, "This dog isn't supposed to be here. We don't allow dogs!"

The concierge, with military posture, strolled over.

He pointed at my black-and-white companion and said in a condescending tone, "That iss not a dog. That is *Doon-can.*"

Duncan had insinuated himself into every aspect of our lives. Many farm dogs live outside because dogs who work in corrals have manure-encrusted paws, and besides, farms have snug barns where dogs and cats can shelter. On top of that, trainers warn against making working dogs into pets. But Duncan was such great company, he became part of everything.

"I've called this meeting to plan the neighborhood circus." Mary, *looking* small in our living room recliner, held a notebook and pencil. "Today we'll figure out the publicity, and after that we'll plan our acts."

Mary's neighborhood friends, two girls named Robin, and Robin Demmer's little brother, Ron, nodded.

"We have to figure out a way to let people know about it," Mary said.

"We can put posters up on the highway!" Robin Preston said.

"We'll call a reporter to come out and do a story on it," Robin Demmer said.

"And put it on the radio," Ron said.

"We're going to have bleachers brought in," Mary said.

"All proceeds will go to charity," Robin P. said.

"I'm going to dance," Mary said, "and do an act with Duncan."

"I'm going to do a high-wire act," Ron said.

"Where?"

"We'll put up a high wire in the front yard."

The committee set a date for a month away, on a Saturday. The kids would give two performances if the yard couldn't accommodate everyone for one show. The circus planners left the meeting with a list of tasks from making tickets to calling the mayor.

"What do you think Duncan should wear?" Mary asked.

"Would he tolerate a hat?"

"I'm thinking about one of my tutus."

When the second planning meeting took place a few days later, a new set of tasks emerged though the first hadn't yet been tackled. I'd watched this before with kids. The fun lay in scheming and dreaming.

Daily, the acts changed. Squabbles arose when a performer balked at doing an act the others wanted him or her to do. At bedtime, Mary recounted the latest plans, disagreements, and grand vision. I and the other moms pointed out the circus date was fast approaching, so it got set back.

"I'm going to have Duncan walk on his back legs," Mary said. "What else?"

I told her about the brief lesson I'd given Duncan in how to go to "place" and jump through a hoop.

Duncan sitting on a stool didn't sound like much of a trick to Mary, but she liked the idea of him going through a hoop. I told her where she could find a thin wooden pole for him to jump over. Her arms were too small for Duncan to jump through, so she'd have to skip that step. She dug out her old hula hoop, and practice for one of the acts actually got under way.

I resolved to stay away from the training so it could be Mary's act, but I offered to help hold the pole. She started Duncan at a very low height—ten inches or so. Duncan hopped over the pole and Mary rewarded him. We lifted the pole higher.

"I think I can do it by myself now."

"Okay."

I watched from the living room window. Mary lifted the pole to thigh level, waist level, and finally to the height of her shoulder. He happily jumped over it each time. She put down the pole and held out her arm. "Over," she said, and he bounded over.

Understandably, she thought he was ready for the hoop. Understandably, he had no idea what she wanted. He'd jumped through my arms a time or two a couple of years before, but that was different from a plastic hoop. When she held up the hoop and told him, "Over," Duncan looked around. He saw nothing to jump. After a few seconds, he lost interest and started watching birds in the trees.

"Duncan. Pay attention." She held up the hoop again.

I'd interfere if I watched longer, so I went off to the kitchen. A few minutes later, Mary came in the house. "Want to see Duncan jump through a hoop?"

"Sure."

Outside, she lifted the hoop, ordered "Over," and Duncan floated through it.

"How'd you get him to do it?"

"At first he didn't know what I meant. But I scolded him and pointed at the hoop. Then he jumped through it." She held up the hoop again. "Duncan. Over." He sailed through.

"Remember to reward him."

"Oh. Yeah." She felt encouraged. "What other tricks can we do? Should I teach him to ride a bike?"

"But you don't know how to ride a bike."

"Well, I guess two tricks will be enough."

One August day, the circus performers noticed that school would start soon. They set the circus for the upcoming Saturday. The scale of things instantly changed, and instead of throngs of spectators, only families would attend.

"Coming to the circus?" I asked Matt and Shane.

They traded a glance.

"Linda Demmer is bringing cookies."

"I guess I could come," Shane said. Matt thought he might, too.

The weather cooperated with lovely blue skies and no wind. The costumed performers gathered beside the trampoline.

Linda Demmer arrived with a container of beautiful cookies. Karen Preston brought a tub of supplies for manufacturing awards for the performers. Wisely, she'd waited to see what acts finally made it to the show. The audience consisted of dads and moms and three older brothers—Matt, Shane, and Robin P.'s older brother, Chris.

Robin P., dressed in a tuxedo, started things out by doing magic tricks. Ron, dressed as a clown, did a series of bike maneuvers—going over jumps, sitting backward on the seat, and riding with hands extended in the air. His dog, Rusty, also in a clown outfit, participated by riding along, his paws on the handlebars.

Mary, in a leather dress and wearing an elk's tooth necklace, did an Indian dance. Robin D., dressed in a princess costume, did a ballet routine. All four kids did tricks on the trampoline—alone or in pairs.

It was time for Mary's act with Duncan. Duncan looked morose. He had stopped trying to get his tutu off after Mary reprimanded him, but he frowned down his slender nose at the net skirt.

Mary told him, "Up." He stood on his hind legs. Mary said, "Walk," and he came forward. She picked up the hula hoop. She told him "Over!" and he leaped through it. Spectators clapped. Mary made him repeat the hoop trick, then she bowed.

Karen fastened rosettes to purple ribbons, sprinkled them with glitter, and lettered them with inscriptions like "Best Bike Act" and "Best Magician." She made a rosette for Duncan with the letters "Best Jumper." She tried to interest him in it, but he turned away, twisted his head over his back, and tried to get hold of the tutu with his teeth.

Though he managed to grab it, he couldn't get rid of it. The circus ended with Duncan sitting by himself, glowering.

DeeDee gazed at the pasture behind the house.

"Is that Shane out there?" DeeDee pushed her glasses higher on her nose. "What is that with him?"

"His pig."

"His *pig*?"

"He walks his pig every day."

After Shane had read in the 4-H hog manual that exercise built good hams and kept pigs lean, he'd started walking his market hogs. The pigs trained easily—a tap from the hog cane on the left shoulder sent them right, a tap on the right shoulder sent them left. If the pig began to root with its snout, Shane hooked the rounded head of the hog cane over the pig's nose and lifted its snout out of the dirt. Then he'd give the pig a tap on its back to get the pig moving again.

He walked his hogs in the corral at first, but that got boring and he decided to try training in the hayfield behind our house. The first time he aimed his hog toward an open gate, the hog gazed at the expanse of open land, let out an ear-splitting squeal, and took off. Shane dashed after it. Watching from the window, I wondered if Shane would ever see the hog again.

Duncan streaked off to get in front of the pig and head it off. He knew how to turn ewes, but the pig kept running. Duncan ran at the pig's head, barking. The pig galloped on. Duncan grabbed the pig's ear and nipped. The pig screamed, opened his mouth, and bit Duncan hard, drawing blood.

But that had been weeks before, and now détente had been reached. Duncan accompanied Shane but walked on the side where the pig wasn't. If the pig took a notion to suddenly streak off, Duncan let Shane handle it. That worked out fine because hogs, at least domestic ones, weren't built for endurance and tired easily when running.

But pigs could manage a long stroll. Shane walked his pigs in the evening after the day cooled, walking first his barrow, the castrated male, and then his gilt, the young female. Duncan went along whenever he wasn't needed to help with evening chores.

I often paused at a window and gazed across the field at a lovely scene. A lean boy with curly black hair, hog cane on his shoulder, sauntered behind a curly-tailed pig. In early summer the pig would be small, but market hogs grow quickly, and soon the pig would be 150 pounds, then 200. As fair time approached, the pig got immense—280 pounds or so. A huge, lumbering hog made the scene slightly less pastoral; still, I wished I knew how to paint. Shane and the pig, in knee-high alfalfa, accompanied by a black-and-white dog, ought to have been captured in oils.

Shane won top prizes at the county fair with his well-toned and muscular pigs, and one year, won champion market hog at the state fair.

But Shane came to want more for his pigs. One evening he came in the house, took off his muddy shoes, and announced, "My gilt likes to herd sheep."

When the kids were little I'd read them *Babe*, the wonderful book about a pig who liked to herd. So I told Shane, "That's been done already."

"No, really. I took Henwen to the sheep pasture for a walk, and she's really interested in the sheep. When she ran after them, they moved away."

"They probably don't like pigs." Shane's old horse Lucy, a completely cooperative animal, balked when I tried to ride her near the hog pens. In summer when Shane had hogs, I had to take her on a round-about path to reach the hill behind our house.

"Henwen wants to turn them and keep them bunched, just like a herding dog."

"Shane." I tilted my head toward Duncan, who was lying on the kitchen rug.

"What? I think Henwen's got talent. We could just try her out the next time we're moving sheep."

"And break a certain someone's heart?"

So Shane gave up the idea of having a herding pig. Duncan had sworn off herding pigs, it was only fair pigs shouldn't herd his sheep.

FIFTEEN

I put the pancakes in a Pyrex dish, set the dish in the oven to stay warm, and went to find George. He'd gone outside as soon as he'd gotten up. I looked in the barn, but neither George nor the sheep were there. I figured he and Duncan must be rounding up the sheep from the pasture, so I went to see if I could help.

The sun sparkled and I felt like breaking into song. But a chilly wind hit me as I came around the barn. I zipped up my jacket all the way and turned up my collar.

I saw George about fifty feet away, with Duncan. The wind carried away George's words, but I heard his angry tone. I saw him pull back his foot and plant a kick in Duncan's side.

Duncan yelped. But he didn't run away. He cowered beside George, ears flattened.

George pulled back his foot and kicked him again. Duncan flopped onto his side and whimpered. George reached over and cuffed him on the head. Duncan cringed.

I stood at the edge of the field, frozen. George saw me then.

"Get up!" he ordered Duncan.

When the dog didn't, George picked him up by his fur and tossed him.

Duncan sidled across the field toward me, everything hanging—ears, head, tail.

"He kept chasing the sheep after I told him to stop!" George's brow had a dark cloud.

"Breakfast," I said, not loud enough to be heard. The ground had opened up, and I stood balanced on the edge of a fissure. I touched

Duncan with the tips of my fingers, turned, and walked toward the house with Duncan slinking beside me. I knew George followed.

At the house I ran my hand over Duncan, checking for injuries. I couldn't find any. I understood that men had different hormones and showed anger more aggressively, but I couldn't chase away the picture of Duncan cowering.

That night, George was sitting at the kitchen table reading the paper when Duncan and I came in from penning sheep.

"Well!" he said, putting down the paper. "How's that best ole doggy in the world doin'?" He leaned over and patted Duncan's head.

Why hadn't Duncan run away? And more to the point, why hadn't I come to Duncan's defense? Why had I stood there like a stick, failing to lift a finger on my dog's behalf?

"I'd like you to come to a Life Training weekend," my friend Mel said.

"Is that a growth event?" I heard a sneer in my voice.

"I guess that's a good description."

"They put people in a room and isolate them from their normal routines? Then people spill their guts to strangers, cry and feel intimate, and are permanently changed?"

"Participants aren't isolated. You go out for meals, you take regular breaks, and you sleep at home."

"I'd rather put that same money into our family vacation fund."

"I'll pay fifty dollars of your registration," Mel offered.

I couldn't help be touched. Mel and Jim had kids in college and lived modestly.

"It's good of you to offer, but I'm not looking for change. I like things the way they are. Besides, I want to be home on weekends."

Though we often had sheep chores to do on Saturday and Sunday, weekends also gave us our only chance for recreation. Sometimes we invited guests for dinner. I liked trying new dishes, making bread, and putting together big salads. George seldom shared in the cooking, but he chopped vegetables, washed pans, and kept the counters clear.

In fall, weekends meant soccer games, two per Saturday because Matt and Shane played on different teams. George and I often split up to cover games. I appreciated George's participation in the kids' activities.

Some autumn days had Indian summer temperatures, but many Saturdays I found myself huddled under a blanket, snowflakes stinging my cheeks, with Duncan snuggled next to me.

Duncan didn't see why he should be excluded from any game involving a ball. The first minutes of a match he'd bark and tug on his leash whenever the ball came past, but after I told him *no*, he'd merely moan and wriggle.

Duncan liked another fall event—Matt's cross-country meets. Duncan came to understand he couldn't run with Matt, but he never stopped giving me a pleading look when runners took off. During a meet, I couldn't distinguish Matt amid a cluster of tall, lanky boys, but Duncan saw Matt the minute a group of runners, small as toys, appeared on the hillside. He would prick his ears, look up at me, and wag.

"There he is!" his look said. "Isn't he fabulous?"

When I strained my eyes, I could make out Matt, moving like a deer with long, easy strides.

In summer, we went camping in the mountains. Duncan enjoyed those outings, though hikes got hectic for him. In his Border collie heart, he believed he needed to keep his humans bunched. So when Matt and Shane ran ahead to scramble up hillsides or climb rocks, Duncan tore after them. When he got ahead of them, he tried to move them back toward us. They ignored him.

"It's okay, Duncan," I called. "They can go ahead." He didn't believe that. He ran a circle around Matt and Shane and tried to push them toward us. His expression said, "Hurry!" Even though he couldn't succeed in keeping family members collected, he wouldn't give up trying.

On weekends, I took time to take Duncan to the field and throw Frisbees for him. Matt, Shane, or Mary often came, too, because one human had no chance of tiring Duncan. We tossed the Frisbee until all of us had sore arms, and still, when we decided to quit, Duncan would persuade us into a few more tosses.

Duncan caught Frisbees with the same élan he chased sprinklers. With great agility, he sprang into the air and grabbed the disk with his teeth. Even a tricky wind that carried the Frisbee first one way and then another, or suspended it in space for a time, couldn't fool Duncan, who kept a sharp eye on the sailing object and managed to snatch it.

In hundreds of tosses Duncan might miss once or twice, and often that wasn't a true miss—just an awkward catch. We didn't have a television, so I'd never seen Frisbee dogs in competition, but people in our 4-H club told us Duncan could have challenged the best of them.

One time at a campground I went to an open area to throw the Frisbee for Duncan. Duncan streaked across the meadow, bounded into the air, grabbed the Frisbee, then dashed back to me. Before long, kids had gathered at the meadow's edge to watch.

Shane came along. "Want me to take a turn?"

"Yeah." I sat down on a log. The kids had gone to their camper and returned with their parents, who waved at us. Aware of the spectators, Shane made it more complicated for Duncan. He threw harder and farther, and in all directions. More people joined the group of onlookers.

Matt walked up and stood beside the log. His eyes scanned the trees and I knew he was studying the wind. "I'll do it awhile," he told Shane.

Matt took over, trying to use the wind direction to make the Frisbee do something unexpected, which was what happened. Duncan watched the Frisbee veer from its course, took a giant sideways leap, and snagged it. Matt grinned at the onlookers, who now numbered about a dozen.

Mary joined in, but she wasn't big enough to do the long, impressive throws that allowed Duncan to make dramatic catches. She gave the Frisbee back to Matt.

Shane had gone over to visit with the spectators. "Never gets tired," I heard him brag, and, "Really good help with our sheep."

We liked an audience. We knew Duncan was the greatest, and it pleased us to have a gathering of people who thought so, too.

Often we took our two canoes to the mountains. We'd found lovely, scenic rivers to float where we saw moose, swans, geese, muskrats, and beaver in the water, rock chucks and deer on the banks, and eagles overhead. I had learned to maneuver arrangements so the outing would produce less strain. George and I did no better maneuvering a canoe than we did working sheep or talking finances.

"Why don't I ride with Shane?" I'd suggest. "That way he can be in the back and practice piloting." Mary and Duncan always rode in the center of the boat.

After having a picnic along the way, we'd return to the canoes.

"Why don't Matt and I ride together?" I'd suggest. "That way he can practice piloting."

But I figured many couples might find paddling a canoe together stressful. Same with working livestock.

So I had no desire to miss out on a future weekend with my family in the interest of "growth." As for the growing list of things George and I didn't do well together, I'd decided the adage "Let sleeping dogs lie" held much wisdom.

SIXTEEN

We didn't hold a memorial service for most ewes, but we did for Syringa.

The five of us stood in a circle around Syringa's body. Duncan joined us and, sensing the solemnity of things, sat stiffly upright. He gazed at each of us in turn, but his "please visit with me" expression was absent.

Matt stared at the ground. Tenderhearted Mary, who often disturbed moviegoers with loud sobbing during sad movies, began to get tearful. Shane set his teenage jaw and folded his arms. George read from John's gospel. " 'The shepherd in charge of the sheep enters by the door. The sheep hear his voice; he calls his own sheep by name, and leads them out. . . . The sheep follow, because they know his voice.' "

My stomach writhed.

Usually when a ewe died, George put her remains in the back of the pickup and drove to a remote location where he left the body as a gift for wild creatures. We would have preferred to take our dead animals to a plant that rendered them to make fat, fertilizer, and feed, but rendering plants in our region no longer accepted sheep carcasses, and the county landfill didn't, either. Though we buried dogs and cats on the place, we couldn't accommodate a graveyard for farm animals.

Fortunately, we didn't lose many ewes. Our Polypays had almost no difficulties when lambing. We vaccinated against serious disease and treated for ovine parasites. We did have cases of mastitis, or hard bag, an inflammation of the udder, which struck our heaviest milking ewes. Syringa was one.

When we'd bought Syringa's mother, Emerald, we'd been novices and saw only that she was elegant. We didn't see what seasoned sheepmen would have—that her delicateness and long swan neck indicated a high presence of female hormones.

Syringa became the most distinguished of the Emerald daughters. Generations later, ewes that carried her genes were great milkers, gave birth to multiples, and had kind dispositions. They even looked like her.

Syringa milked like a Holstein and dragged around a bag engorged with milk, which made it more susceptible to infection. One year she got mastitis, and though we treated her with antibiotics, one side of her bag froze solid and became unusable. Despite that, the next year Syringa raised two of her three lambs on one teat, and at weaning time, those two lambs showed the best weight gain.

Then she got mastitis on the other side, too. Sheep raisers often sold off ewes who couldn't raise their own lambs, but we didn't consider getting rid of Syringa. We raised her lambs on bottles, but she helped by hovering over them and keeping them warm on chilly nights.

Then she developed cancer eye. The treatment turned out to be a lye-based product that we sprinkled into her eye. It ate away the cancer and also destroyed the eye. It must have been horribly painful when we administered the powder, but she never became hard to catch or treat.

George found her dead one warm summer morning.

At our service, we each spoke of some connection we had to her. I remembered her friendliness. Shane recalled that two of his high-placing market lambs had been her offspring. Mary, who had just become a 4-H'er, pointed out that her young ewe, Marsha Veronica, was Syringa's daughter. Matt pointed out that the best rams we'd raised were Syringa's sons. George said we owed the overall quality of our flock to Syringa.

Mary placed wild buttercups from our lower pasture on Syringa's snowy head and then George and Shane loaded her body into the pickup.

I stayed in the shade by the lambing shed, stomach twisted with grief. Duncan made no attempt to move; he sat next me, still as a stone. I reached down and fondled his ears. "Be careful. I couldn't handle a funeral for you."

I didn't seem to be getting tougher. I wondered if I ever would. Watching animals die still made me miserable.

SEVENTEEN

At Idaho's Redfish Lake, we'd come to the water's edge to view the peaks and crystalline water at dusk. We'd spent the afternoon canoeing and now George was taking a nap and the kids and I had taken Duncan for a walk.

Matt and Shane picked up stones to skip on the water. Mary knelt in the meadow grass, sniffing yellow heart-leafed arnica and pink columbines. Farther down the beach, a man was getting ready to throw an inflated cylinder.

We watched the man draw back his arm, then hurl the float. It fell on the lake's surface with a plunk. The man's black Labrador leaped into the water, paddled to the floating object, grabbed it in his teeth, and swam to shore.

"That man's training his dog for hunting," I told Mary.

Duncan, ears perked, watched the dog come out of the water and return to the man. When the man leaned over and praised the Lab, Duncan looked up at me with an expression of delight.

The man drew his arm back again and threw the float hard. It soared over the lake and landed a long way out. Duncan streaked off.

"Duncan!" I yelled, but he had already leaped into the lake and started to swim toward the float. He was smaller than the muscular Lab, but he moved with great purpose.

The Lab looked surprised to see Duncan swimming toward his toy, so he sped up. So did Duncan. The Lab lost some momentum by intermittently checking out where Duncan was. Duncan paid no attention to the Lab.

The Lab, who had less distance to swim, was about to seize the float when Duncan slipped in from the side and cut him off. Duncan

grabbed the float in his mouth and turned for shore. Looking be-
wildered, the Lab paddled after him.

Shane came over to join Mary and me. "Shouldn't that big dog be
faster than Dunc?"

"I bet he's warmer, too. Labradors have water-resistant under-
coats."

Duncan reached the beach, ran to the owner, and dropped the
float at his feet. The owner glanced our way and frowned.

"Duncan!" I hollered. "Come!"

Duncan sped toward us.

Shane congratulated Duncan. "Duncan, that dog has had practice. You just watched once and understood."

I held Duncan by the collar when the man hurled the float again.
Duncan whimpered.

"Let's go," I said. Joined by Shane, we started walking. "Heel," I
told Duncan, and he did.

We climbed an incline to a forested place that gave us an even
wider view. While ogling scenery I didn't notice the man winding up
to throw the float. But Duncan did. When the cylinder hit the water,
Duncan leaped off the ridge, hit the water with a thud, and started
paddling.

This time the Lab saw Duncan coming. He paddled furiously, but
I thought he had little to worry about; Duncan had too much distance to cover.

Duncan glided through the water like an otter, but he couldn't get
there in time. The Lab seized the float. But unlike the Lab, who had
become perturbed when Duncan got the float first, Duncan stayed
smooth and confident. He swam alongside the Lab as both dogs
headed back to the beach.

We were too far away to see exactly what happened, but it appeared that Duncan either hit or nipped the Lab on his backside, and
when the Lab turned to look, Duncan snatched the float. Then Duncan calmly swam on, undistracted by the Lab, who kept lunging at
the toy.

The dog owner looked up at the rise where we were standing. He raised his hand.

"Wave!" I ordered, hoping the man's gesture had been friendly.

The man went forward to meet the dogs, but Duncan raced past him. The Lab followed Duncan for a second, then returned to his master and plunked down in disappointment. It hadn't been lost on Duncan that he'd received no praise for his efforts the first time, so he ran to us with his trophy.

Shane asked, "Should we tell him he's bad?"

"He disobeyed," I said.

But we couldn't find the heart to scold him. "Clever guy," we said quietly. Mary couldn't stop giggling. Matt, grinning, caught up with us. "Did you see that?" he asked.

We made our faces sober and met the man halfway. "I'm sorry," I said, handing him the float.

The man pointed at the dripping Duncan. "Smart dog." Duncan sat down beside the man and gazed up with hopeful goodwill. The man crossed his arms over his chest and studied first Duncan, then his own dog, who was being showered with attention from Matt, Shane, and Mary.

He scowled at all of us and walked off. Duncan didn't make many social faux pas, but he had this time.

Usually, Duncan shone as a diplomat. Twice each month, twenty-five kids, often accompanied by parents, came to our house for 4-H livestock meetings to give their demonstrations, discuss club business, and plan for the August fair. As animals of unfamiliar scent lined up on his front lawn or were carried in cages to the basement, Duncan exhibited no territorialism or jealousy. During our annual practice show, he was allowed to trot alongside the judge, acting as a sort of canine ring steward as the judge inspected kids and animals.

Amber, a pudgy girl with a tangle of curly brown hair, arrived carrying a small hutch with a small brown rabbit in it.

"For my demonstration, I'm going to show how to train a rabbit for the fair." Amber had a squeaky, excited voice.

Duncan peered into the hutch.

"Will Duncan scare Carmella?"

"Not intentionally."

Our 4-H'ers ranged in age from eight to nineteen. If they lived in subdivisions where livestock was forbidden, as Amber did, they enrolled in projects like rabbits or veterinary medicine. If they lived on acreages, they usually chose sheep projects; if they lived on farms and ranches they could take projects ranging from dairy to hog, market beef to breeding cattle.

In a few minutes, the basement was overflowing. Zack, a high school junior with bleached hair announced, "I bring this meeting of the New Sweden Livestock 4-H club to order. Gene, you lead the 4-H pledge; Anjie, the Pledge of Allegiance."

Everyone stood but Duncan, who sat at attention while we pledged allegiance to the flag and then pledged our heads to clearer thinking; hearts to greater loyalty; hands to larger service, and health to better living for our club, our community, our country, and our world.

Rita, a bossy eighth grader, read the minutes. Hailie, a first-year member, whispered, "Here, Duncan." A shy girl, Hailie had not yet found a group to join. She threw her arm around Duncan and pulled him close.

We lacked seating for everyone so parents got the first chance at chairs. The kids usually sprawled on the floor in groups of three or four with others their same age.

Duncan, at this moment, was not free to move, but he took it in good stride. I knew that when Hailie relaxed her hold for a minute, he would trot off to the next person. And that's what happened.

"Duncan, come back!" Hailie pleaded. Duncan acknowledged her with an over-the-shoulder smile but kept going. Duncan made sure he spent a few minutes with each child and adult guest. Because of the floor seating and because kids didn't stay in one place very long, it would have been understandable if Duncan became confused about whom he had visited. But he had an accountant's mind for detail and he kept track of everyone, no matter how they moved about. I never saw him overlook anyone or visit someone twice.

Duncan sat down in front of Rick, a freckled boy, and gazed at him. Rick was busy whispering to Greg. Duncan thrust his head closer.

Greg hit Rick on the arm. "Duncan wants to say hi."

"Hi." Rick gave Duncan a pat and went on talking.

That wasn't Duncan's idea of visiting. He sat his ground, waiting.

"Duncan, what do you want, attention? Okay, how's this?" Rick rubbed Duncan's head. "How you been, buddy?"

After this exchange, Duncan moved to the next person, a dad seated on the floor who was gazing at the ceiling. Duncan touched his nose to the man's hand. Only after the father acknowledged him did Duncan move on.

By the time Duncan had completed his rounds, two demonstrations had been given. Amber stepped to the front of the room with the wire hutch and Carmella.

"The name of my demonstration is 'How to Train a Rabbit for the Fair.' "

Greg turned to Rick and did a not-very-quiet mimic of a squeaky voice.

Amber removed Carmella from the cage and set the rabbit on the table. "This is how you teach a rabbit to be quiet for judging." Amber smoothed the rabbit from nose to tail, arranging its ears flat over its back.

Duncan's rounds were complete, so he could return to a favorite person. Sometimes he came back to me, Matt, Shane, or Mary, but he had a sense for who needed special attention, and went and sat next to Lamar, who was eleven. Lamar had received a brain injury as a child and had difficulty speaking. Lynne, my coleader and I, had hoped he might have a positive experience with his animal, a lamb, but so far he'd made no friends in the club and had stayed remote from activities. One time, he had burst into hot tears for no reason we could see.

Lately, Duncan had spent most 4-H meetings with Lamar. Lamar's mother told me her son never sat still for long but could manage it when Duncan was next to him. Tonight, Lamar's eyes darted and his hands fidgeted. Duncan leaned against him. Lamar took hold of Duncan's collar but stared at a space on the wall.

Lamar got up. So did Duncan. Lamar, holding the railing, clumped up the stairs. Duncan clung to his heels. Lynne and I traded a look. We kept our places. Lamar sometimes wandered around upstairs, then returned. Our house offered few hazards; I didn't believe Lamar could get hurt.

Amber had just turned Carmella the bunny on its back and was demonstrating how to display a rabbit's teeth for a judge when Duncan dashed into the room and ran to me. I jumped up and followed him upstairs.

"Let's give Amber our full attention," I heard Lynne order.

I found Lamar on the front porch, staring at the road, forehead wrinkled.

"What's wrong? Can I help you?"

Duncan squeezed against Lamar's leg.

"Duncan's right here, and your mom will be back in a few minutes. There's nothing to worry about." Russian olive trees exhaling into the evening sent a healing fragrance our way, but Lamar remained tense. He couldn't tell me what was wrong. I guided him back into the house, but he wouldn't go downstairs. He sat upstairs at the kitchen table, petting Duncan and wearing a nervous look until it was time for refreshments.

At a 4-H meeting the following month, Duncan surprised me. After he made his rounds, he chose to sit next to Sarah, though Lamar was again fidgety and distracted. Sarah, ten, was new to the club but had instantly made friends with three other girls.

Lamar spent much of the meeting wandering upstairs—we heard his clunking footsteps above us, but Duncan didn't leave once to check on him. I watched Duncan snuggle close to Sarah and wondered if I had imagined his sensitivity. Or maybe Duncan had given up on Lamar and decided to throw in with more regular kids. I frowned across the room at him, though I, too, felt over my head with Lamar.

Even during refreshments, Duncan stuck with Sarah while she chatted with her friends. Only when people went outside and started to move trucks and trailers so they could load their animals did Duncan dash outside to help. He circled the trailers, rushing at the heels of any animal that didn't want to load.

Almost everyone had left when Sarah's mother motioned for me to follow her to the porch. When we got there she said, "I wanted to tell you . . ." and burst into tears.

Sarah's little sister had been in the hospital fighting a deadly infection. The girl had come through it all right, but it had been a nightmare for the family.

When I went back to the yard to help a boy load his lambs, I looked down at Duncan and asked, "How is it you know?"

He dashed past me, heading for a ewe that looked like she might try to escape his watchful eye.

EIGHTEEN

·····················

I came in from doing chores and found George hunched over the newspaper. As I removed my soiled shoes, I peered over to see what he was reading. It was the classified section.

"Whatcha looking at?"

"Nothing."

I stretched my neck and saw he had circled some ads.

I went to the computer to work. When I came back to the kitchen to start supper, I found the classified section with circled ads on the counter beside the phone. George had marked advertisements for small acreages or farms within twenty-five miles.

When I picked up my paring knife, my hand shook. A small farm, to accommodate a single man? Was George looking to move? During arguments he often threatened to leave, but I would jump in with a list of reasons why he mustn't—the kids, the farm, our commitment. As far as I knew, we weren't in conflict now, but maybe we hadn't solved an old upset.

Circling ads and calling about them struck me as dire. I couldn't fail again. And I didn't want the kids to endure the pain of a family breakup.

I wondered if I had the courage to ask George about the ads. Probably not. And maybe I didn't want an answer. Instead, I could step very lightly and try to avoid future conflicts.

Laron, the minister at the Methodist Church, had come for dinner and I was showing him around the place. Duncan, ever gracious as a host, trotted close beside Laron, smiling up frequently.

"This is Hawk," I said, stopping at the ram pen. "He's a honey."

"A honey," Laron repeated. "What does that mean?"

"He's tall, a quadruplet by birth, and has great length. See?" I showed Laron the distance between Hawk's neck and hip, and hip and tail. "His daughters are highly productive and beautiful. They all have wonderful dispositions, like him." Because I was talking to a pastor, I didn't mention Hawk's astonishing testicles, which always drew comments from sheep raisers.

Laron reached out to pet Hawk.

"Don't touch him."

"You said he was nice."

"He is. But if you pet him, your hands will stink."

"I remember that about sheep. People say they stink."

"Hawk stinks because he's our breeding ram. He has a musky scent that is hard to wash off. But we think sheep have a nice scent."

"I have a hard time giving sermons on sheep passages in the Bible because people say sheep are dumb."

"Sit down." I ordered Laron to a hay bale, ignoring his dapper pants. He was about to be preached to. People who raise sheep, I said, realize they are the most misunderstood of animals. Stereotypes about them include: they are always looking for a place to die; they follow a leader mindlessly; they are passive to the point of lacking survival instincts; they are dumber than mud; and they are destructive to the land.

"And they all look alike," Laron said. "How can you know them by name?"

"We'll get to that."

About being stinky, I began: "When producers ran sheep in great numbers in the West, sheep bed grounds carried a distinctive scent. When cattle came along behind them, the cattle reacted to the smell. Cowboys complained. But it isn't unusual for one species to dislike the smell of another. Most animals—horses, dogs, cattle, and hogs—and wild varieties like elk and bear, have distinctive scents."

"I think a city bus crowded with people doesn't smell very good,"

Laron said. "What about the cowboy's complaint that sheep ruined the land?"

"That was true. Before the Taylor Grazing Act, sheepmen allowed their animals to overgraze the land to ruination. Sheep crop the grass short, but if moved frequently, sheep improve the land. Unlike cattle, who leave cow pies that nothing can grow under, sheep fertilize the land with high-nutrient pellets that the land quickly absorbs."

Laron glanced toward the house, perhaps wondering about dinner.

"On top of that, sheep bed down on ridges so they can catch a breeze. On grazing allotments, they're easier on riparian areas because they don't hang around creeks like cattle do."

Laron sniffed the air. "Is that stew I smell?"

"I'm not done," I said. "It's true that sheep follow each other. Sticking together can be good survival behavior for prey animals. But it's a trait that gets them into trouble sometimes, as it does humans."

About their supposed frailness, I told Laron what a manager of the U.S. Sheep Experiment Station had told me. "Sheep, more than any other domesticated animal, respond to the care they receive. If well cared for, they almost can't be killed. But if poorly shepherded, they go into rapid decline and contract all kinds of ailments. Doesn't that prove they're a sensitive species?" I asked.

"I'm sorry I said they stink. Can we eat now?"

"About them stinking . . ."

"I said I was sorry. . . ."

"Sulfur compounds from food usually go into an animal's manure and make it smelly. In sheep, the sulfur goes into growing wool. Therefore, sheep manure doesn't have a strong odor."

Laron gazed at me. He was a busy bachelor minister, an intellectual with city roots who grabbed meals on the fly and probably wanted only a home-cooked meal.

I felt a special affection for Laron. Our family had started attending the Methodist church because of their strong youth program, but Laron had attracted a following of people who came to hear his eloquent sermons. He nearly always spoke on the same topic. Grace. A person didn't have to do anything to earn God's love, Laron stressed, and nothing a person did could dispel God's love. I loved the idea intellectually, but I had a hard time believing it in my gut. Deep down, I suspected God kept track of my misdeeds, watching for a chance to swoop down and punish me. I desired a more mature understanding of the divine, but I couldn't seem to get rid of the old one.

On one occasion after church I'd told Laron, "If you keep preaching about grace, I might finally get it."

He'd answered, "If I keep preaching about grace, *I* might finally get it."

Now I studied him, looking uncomfortable on his hay bale seat. "So, you want to go eat?"

"I'm not quite as hungry as before."

I'd probably dampened his appetite with my discourse on manure.

He did eat like a bird compared to the five of us, who were fast and competitive eaters, but Laron insisted he hadn't eaten so much in ages.

Unfortunately for Laron, George's topic of conversation happened to be sheep, and what wonderful animals they were.

After supper, Laron said, "I'm still puzzled, how do you tell them apart?"

I took him to a pen of ewes and pointed out differences in body types and facial features in some of my favorite ewes—Topaz, Ladybug, Swallow, Syringa, Daisy, and Rachel. In a few minutes, Laron started being able to identify them.

"That's Topaz, with the square face! And this one is . . . Syringa? With the pleading eyes?"

"Correct."

As evenings go, I don't suppose it rated as the most sophisticated or cultural for Laron that season. Yet, a couple of months later in church, when the scripture lesson was the beautiful passage from John 10 about a shepherd who calls his sheep by name and the sheep who recognize the shepherd's voice, Laron gave an affecting sermon, mentioning Daisy, Syringa, and Topaz like they were old friends.

A year or so later, Laron would leave Idaho Falls to go to a urban area where he could find better medical care for AIDS and greater tolerance as he faced death. I got it then, why he'd so frequently spoken about grace. It would take me awhile longer to figure out my own deep craving for grace.

In my day-to-day life, I continually observed the ways sheep disproved their reputation of being stupid.

When sheep-raiser friends visited, they could walk among our sheep and our sheep scarcely noticed them. Yet, when others visited, even people I knew to be animal lovers, the sheep fled. Maybe sheep raisers carried the scent of sheep on them. Maybe sheep raisers telegraphed they were comfortable with sheep. Whatever the reason, I noticed our sheep were alert to the difference.

In spring, we set up creep feeders—tubs full of grain—lambs had access to at all times. We created barriers that ewes couldn't fit through because we didn't want them getting into the grain and overeating. Lambs had to thread their way down an alley and go under a panel to find their way to an open area where we placed the grain.

If we set up the maze in the morning, the lambs would have it figured out by noon and be congregated around the grain. I had set up creep feeder mazes for colts, too, but the colts took longer to figure them out.

Everyone held that sheep were passive, but sheep raisers could tell stories of ewes that tried to hold off coyotes or dogs that were attacking their lambs. Nature had not equipped them to do it, but they died trying.

I admired sheep for their splendid mothering. In years of raising sheep, we could count on the fingers of one hand the ewes who had rejected their young. Many, in fact, happily raised lambs they hadn't given birth to.

Sheep were hardier than their reputations gave them credit for. "Sheep have a reputation for dying suddenly because they endure so much before making a first complaint," a veterinarian had told me. "They are incredibly stoic." We ourselves had seen ewes and lambs pull through grave diseases and injuries, showing great heart and desire to live.

I appreciated our ewes for their tranquil natures, too. And I came to admire the friendships I saw develop among them.

Daisy and Swallow were a year apart in age and therefore did not grow up together. They became friends when they were jugged side by side in the lambing barn. Daisy was a two-year-old; Swallow was a yearling. After we turned the ewes out, Daisy and Swallow continued to hang around together.

Both came from our best families. Daisy's line, along with being productive, tended to be beautiful. Daisy had almost perfect conformation, wide loin, straight legs with good bone, and an attractive head. She went to the Eastern Idaho State Fair every year, always winning first in her class and, as a four-year-old, won Champion Polypay Ewe.

Swallow belonged to Shane, and she raised the sturdiest, fastest-growing lambs on the place. Shane chose the lamb he would raise as his 4-H project from his own flock rather than from the bigger herd. Swallow wasn't impressive in looks and didn't go to fairs. When Daisy was away winning beauty pageants, Swallow moped.

Every year, the two friends managed to lamb within a day of each other, often within hours. If one of them lambed, we started watching the other for signs of labor. In the lambing barn, if one of their lambs strayed into the neighboring jug, its mother's friend would nurse it and make it feel at home.

Swallow, the strictest ewe in the flock, kept her lambs at her side and didn't allow them to run and play. If Swallow had been a range ewe, her lambs would have had the best chance for survival because they were every minute under her watchful eye. She raised to maturity every lamb she gave birth to. But Swallow's lambs didn't grow up without playmates, because Daisy stayed close to Swallow, bringing her lambs along.

When their lambs were weaned, Daisy and Swallow would move to summer pasture behind the house. I could see them from the kitchen window, the two of them moving in tandem over the rise, nibbling grass a little distance from the rest of the flock.

One year, Daisy became piteously thin after lambing. Over her strenuous protests, we took away two of her lambs and raised them on bottles to lessen the stress on her. We left her one lamb so she wouldn't be completely distraught.

Swallow waited patiently beside the shed for Daisy to be let out. After we turned Daisy out, Swallow stayed close by her friend's side, though Daisy spent much time lying down. We gave Daisy antibiotics, and I fed her additional portions of grain. But by the time we weaned lambs and put the ewes in the summer pasture, Daisy still looked thin and weak. One afternoon, I found her dead under a shade tree. Swallow stood beside her.

Heavy-hearted, I returned to the house for a rope to drag her away. When I got back, Swallow wasn't around. I looked for her among ewes shaded up under the shed, but she wasn't there. I found her in a sunny patch of grass, eyes glazed, trembling like it was cold. I checked her for injuries and couldn't find any. She didn't show signs of bloat or weed poisoning. I tried without success to coax her to her feet. I went back to the house to get Duncan—he could persuade her to move. When I returned, Swallow was dead.

Some people would say sheep aren't capable of higher emotions. For me, Daisy and Swallow illustrated that sheep could form bonds that pushed down even the great separating wall of death. Down the road, when I began to wonder if love might be a fiction people had made up, I'd recall the example of devotion I'd seen in supposedly lower animals, and that would hearten me.

NINETEEN

I appreciated Duncan's sensitivity to 4-H kids but felt less pleased when he befriended strangers of the down-on-their-luck variety.

I loved the Idaho Falls Greenbelt, a pedestrian path with colorful flower beds and a view of the tumbling river. As summer days shortened and evenings got cooler, white anemone and orange and lavender mums bloomed furiously. Transients who lived under the bridge clung to the banks awhile longer, too. I often felt a pang when I saw a man lying under newspapers, holey shoes sticking out. But I wanted to walk past without meeting him. Duncan had other ideas.

"Duncan, no!" I tugged on him. He ignored me. Strong as a bull, he pulled me toward the napping man. "Stop!" I hissed.

When we got there, Duncan sat down courteously. He would not waken someone who wanted to remain asleep.

I whispered, *"Duncan, come on!"*

He pretended he didn't hear. Beneath the yellowed paper, snoring continued.

Duncan, can't you smell the liquor?

If he couldn't get a response, Duncan would stop tugging and we would stride off. Then Duncan would run at me in a false attack, trying to get me to play.

"Don't try to be charming. You were very stubborn," I'd scold.

Sometimes a man looked out from the edge of a paper and scowled at the dog who'd materialized at his side. Other times, a homeless man or woman would take hold of Duncan's collar like they'd found a life belt.

"Thank you for coming to see me. Thank you," a haggard woman said to him.

Duncan would look at me with reproach. "Did you see that marvelous person I just met?"

One evening, I paused to look at the falls. A man and woman stood nearby, gazing at the churning water. The woman looked over and noticed Duncan.

"What a beautiful dog!" She all but fell atop him. "Isn't he pretty?" she exclaimed to her companion, who gave a surly nod.

Tattoos of snakes and sea monsters covered the woman's neck, arms, and legs, and her straw hair was tangled. I studied the man and wondered if he had some responsibility for the woman's missing teeth.

"What's the dog's name?" the woman asked.

"Duncan."

"Duncan? That's *perfect.*" The woman sat down on the concrete overlook and began rubbing Duncan's ears. He lay on his back, giving her his stomach. She started rubbing his tummy, too roughly, I thought. I wondered if she was high.

"Come on, Duncan," I said.

The woman's face drooped. "Are you going?"

"We need to keep walking," I said.

Duncan didn't move.

"Come, Duncan," I said.

He remained on his back. Duncan, who loved walking the greenbelt, had decided to remain where he was. For an interminable ten minutes, the woman lavished affection on him while I tried to get him back, though my better nature suspected the woman carried a sadness Duncan had tuned into.

After we left, I mumbled to Duncan, "Could we be more selective in the future?"

He looked over his shoulder at the pair, who were walking toward their car. The woman's back sagged.

Duncan gave me a stern look.

"Or, I could be less judgmental."

He didn't know how to bestow tenderness selectively. Good thing, because I had come to depend on his indiscriminate kindness.

TWENTY

My kitchen window looked out on farmland, and that made for happy meal preparation. Tasks like scraping carrots or mixing muffins were transformed from tedious to transcendental. I had a view of blue mountains to the south, puffy clouds agglomerating in the west, and white balls of sheep rolling over silver-green pasture. Next to the sheep pasture, the alfalfa field glistened with droplets from being freshly irrigated.

Duncan lay at my feet as I chopped celery and dumped it into the frying pan. George had gone outside to get our teaser ram out of the pasture and replace him with our fertile ram. It was August, and we were exposing our mature ewes so we'd have January lambs that would finish in time for the Easter and Passover market.

For years we had been using a teaser, or vasectomized, ram. For some reason, the presence of a ram in their midst brought all the ewes into heat. Our veterinarian had given our old ram Jasper a vasectomy when we could no longer use him for breeding because many of our ewes were related to him. We put him in with our ewes through a breeding cycle, then we replaced him with a fertile ram. The ewes bred up quickly, which shortened our lambing time. This method worked so well we often were done with lambing in three weeks, while some sheep raisers we knew had lambing seasons that lasted months, which meant a long time of getting up at night for barn checks. Our friends started asking to borrow Jasper, and though sheep get attached to their homes, I suppose the change of scenery did him good.

From my window, I watched George take Jasper out of the field with ewes and put him into a pen with ram lambs. If the rams had been older, they would have challenged the mature ram. Whenever we put two mature rams together, we doused them with vinegar to camouflage their smell; otherwise, they would fight. When rams butted heads, the clash could be heard for a long way, and one might get killed.

George caught our fertile ram, Orion, in his pen, tied him to the fence, and fitted a red crayon on to the breeding harness. Wearing the harness and crayon, Orion would leave a red mark on the back of the ewes he mounted. We recorded when a ewe was marked so we'd know when she would lamb.

A few weeks before, we'd put our ewes on a high-nutrition diet. We liked to have our ewes on the gain, but not overly fat, when they conceived, because that increased the chance of multiples. Orion looked a bit fat, but he'd lose weight when he started chasing ewes and forgot to eat.

I saw George struggling to fit the breeding harness on Orion. Orion, full of male hormones and his own opinions, leaped into the air and struggled to escape. Finally, the ram succeeded in pulling the rope loose. He bolted. George caught hold of the rope as the ram sped past. Stopping Orion in mid-flight almost pulled George off his feet. Red crayon smeared his hands and arms. He dropped the harness.

George yanked the ram toward him. When he got within reach, he kicked Orion in the head. I winced. But I needn't have. Rams have heads of steel. George let out a yell that carried to the house, grabbed his cowboy-booted foot, and began to hop in a circle.

Maybe George had broken a toe. He'd kicked what amounted to a slab of granite.

Orion, dragging the rope, dashed to the horse corral. He'd have to be caught again, but it wouldn't be hard because he was a sucker for a grain bucket.

In the meantime, George danced around, yowling, cussing, and clutching his foot.

"Mom?"

I looked over. Mary, curly hair a snarled mess from playing out in the wind, had come into the kitchen without me noticing.

"What's funny?"

"Nothing!" I wiped the grin off my face. I put a new celery stalk on the cutting board and sliced it down the middle.

"You were looking out the window and laughing."

"I was?" I assumed a sober face. "Well, there's nothing funny out there."

George came into view again, hopping in a circle like an aboriginal dancer, his arms decorated with red streaks. In my head, I heard an accompanying drumbeat.

I glanced down to see if Mary still stood beside me. She'd left.

I gazed out the window again and this time, let myself laugh out loud.

Fall

TWENTY-ONE

Idaho's U.S. Sheep Experiment Station and private breeders had started experimenting with reduced light and its effect on breeding.

Sheep naturally mate in the fall, so researchers manipulated how much light animals were exposed to, to make animals think fall had arrived. Ewes and rams confined to a darkened barn for a certain number of hours per day became fertile. The research was driven by a desire to make lamb available year round in the grocery stores.

The experiments involved other breeds, not Polypays, which already had an extended breeding season. We'd had lambs born on our place during every month of the year.

If we bred ewes in August, we got mostly twins and some triplets in January. We would then rebreed those mothers for summer lambing. If we waited for the sheep's natural breeding time and bred in October, we got triplets and quadruplets in March, which gave us almost as many lambs as the other method. We vacillated on which system to favor; lambing in January could be brutal, but March had its share of high winds and blizzards, too. In years when Midwestern breeders paid high prices for ewes that were proven out-of-season breeders, we catered to that market and put our ewes on the so-called twice-a-year lambing schedule. (The ewes actually produced three lamb crops in two years.)

Light/darkness studies on humans had my attention, too; the ones about the effect of daylight on depression. I had come to dread fall. As hours of darkness increased, George, too, became darker. I wondered if he connected fall with his father's suicide or if something physiological kicked in. I tried to wish the gloominess away, but pretending sometimes wasn't possible.

I came home from town and found George in the bedroom, packing. Two suits lay on the bed, along with socks, underwear, and an open suitcase.

"Where are you going?"

"I don't know."

"What about the family?"

"I wasn't meant to be married."

"It's a little late for that, isn't it?" My voice rose to a hysterical pitch.

He closed the suitcase, picked up the suits, and walked from the bedroom.

I waited a few hours for him to return, then starting calling motels. My head throbbed and my belly ached. I tried several places before I found him. "Don't do this," I pleaded. He came home.

It happened too often. He threatened to leave, and I begged him not to. Afterward, he sometimes felt remorseful, and I always felt resentful. I never considered that I played a role in this drama.

Fall now brought two consuming activities my way. One was helping to get the sheep ready to breed—flushing them on pasture, worming and vaccinating, and checking ewes for health problems. My other effort was futile—trying to hold back the increasing hours of darkness.

Mel called.

"Another Life Training weekend will be held here. I'd so much like to have you come."

"Thanks, but I don't think so."

"I've been talking to my friend Mark." Mark was a concert pianist I admired and a Life Training graduate. "He told me to tell you the weekend would make you a better writer."

"No fair, Mel." Now I had to think about it.

The following month, on a Friday afternoon, I said good-bye to Mary and George and went to the motel where the Life Training weekend would occur. Matt was off at a debate tournament, Shane at a band competition. They were high school seniors.

People pasting on name tags looked as diffident as I. I wished I were gazing out my kitchen window or reading with Mary.

Anne, the trainer, welcomed us and asked, "Would you like to be more awake? Less reactive? Would you like to notice what messages your mind gives you and learn to discern whether those messages are true?"

The introductory talk sounded fairly general, but I noticed my stomach starting to churn. I went to the restroom and doubled over with pain. I had flu symptoms, but I sensed it wasn't the flu. I would have gone home right then, but Mel had paid part of my tuition as a gift, and I felt bound to stay.

Early Saturday morning, someone sat down in a chair I'd pulled up for myself. I apologized and found myself another one. A few minutes later, a trainee came in late. When Anne commented on that, I volunteered I might be to blame because I'd told him about a parking area located far from the meeting room.

Anne came over and asked me to stand.

"Is it your habit to apologize for things that aren't your fault?" she asked.

"No," I said. But I noticed Mel, leaning against the back wall, nodding.

It was the kind of overly analytical question I might have expected in this setting. But when I glanced at the side of the room, a couple of other people I knew were nodding vigorously.

Anne asked me another question, but I found myself drifting out of the room.

She put her hand on my arm. "How old do you feel at this moment?"

An answer popped out. "Five."

"What are you wearing?" she asked.

I surprised myself. "A gray uniform."

"Where are you?"

"The orphanage," I said.

"Why are you there? Are you an orphan?"

"No! I'm waiting for my mother to come and get me."

"When is she coming?"

It was a sacred principle with me, I did not cry in public. Yet, I felt my eyes getting wet.

"When is your mother coming?" Anne asked again.

Couldn't see she was making me cry? I slapped away tears. I wished she wouldn't be so relentless.

"Where do you sleep?" She asked the question in the present tense.

"In a ward with lots of kids."

"Are you friends with them?"

I told her I wasn't friends with them because they cried at night and wet the bed. I didn't, because I wasn't a real orphan.

She asked if I had siblings. I told her my older sister, Bobbette, was there, too.

"Do you get to see her?"

"The other day . . ." I stopped, realizing how ridiculous it was to speak of an episode that happened decades before as "the other day."

"I mean, one time—"

"The other day," Anne corrected. "Stay right there."

I could see them like it was yesterday. From my hiding spot behind the kitchen door, I saw Bobbette and the girls from her floor coming to the lunchroom, wearing uniforms and sacks on their heads. An outbreak of ringworm meant they'd had to have their heads shaved. I couldn't remember if I'd gotten to speak with Bobbette.

"Did your mother ever come for you?"

"Yes!" See? We shouldn't make too much of this, because after all, I wasn't a real orphan. A bed-wetting, sniveling real orphan.

"Did you ever get sent away again?"

I stared at her. "What?"

"Did you ever get sent away again?"

I knew I shouldn't have come to this weekend where a nosy stranger insisted on dredging up a past long gone and best forgotten.

In my present life I never gave any thought to my childhood and I didn't discuss it with even close friends.

"Did you ever get sent away again?"

I tried to scowl at Anne. Instead, my hands came up to hide my face and I began to weep.

Anne held my shoulder. "Is that a yes?"

Time after time. But I never got used to it. Always, it took me by surprise. I would go for a drive with my mother. When we arrived at a house, often my grandmother's, sometimes my uncle's, sometimes the home of a complete stranger, my mother would whip out a suitcase from the car's trunk. My stay might be weeks or months.

"How do you keep from getting sent away now?"

I stared at her. "What?"

"How?"

"I, um, work hard. I try not to be any trouble. I don't say what I'm really thinking."

As the weekend went on, other team members took me through exercises aimed at helping me see how my childhood impacted my present life. I failed to set boundaries, then felt resentful or victimized. I didn't challenge the opinions of others, afraid they'd get mad at me. My self-imposed ban on tears evaporated and to my great humiliation, I cried almost the whole time.

One team member pushed me to look at how my frightened outlook affected me as a marriage partner. I confessed I didn't know even basic things about our finances.

"Are you content to be a child in your marriage?" the man asked.

"I concern myself with the kids, sheep, and writing." But it took me only a minute to reconsider.

"No."

On Sunday night, I made a commitment to the group.

"I'm going to start behaving like an adult in my marriage." The others made me repeat it until it came out audibly. Then they applauded.

My mind raced ahead to other things I might give up. I could quit underplaying my intelligence, stop worrying whether a smart me might threaten others. I could stop being inconspicuous. When I'd lived with my mother, I'd kept a low profile. If I wasn't seen, I wouldn't get hit and I might not get sent away. It had served as a good strategy then, but being inconspicuous didn't help me now. In groups, I spoke too softly to be heard. As the author of three books, I received invitations to speak to groups and on those occasions delivered overrehearsed talks in a mousy voice.

I saw now why I quailed whenever George declared he was quitting the marriage. I wondered if I could remain an adult the next time he threatened and not turn into a five-year-old. I wondered if I could let him choose to go.

TWENTY-TWO

"I've been thinking"—I stopped and took a breath—"that I ought to learn more about our money."

"Like what?"

"Like how much money you make. And how much we have in the bank. If we have any stocks."

George swigged the last of his coffee. "You want to see a pay stub?"

"Yes." I gave a toothpaste commercial smile, striving to be ingratiating.

"I'll show you one my next pay period."

"Fine." It hurt to smile so forcefully. "I'd like to take over paying the household bills, too."

He gave me a long look. Then he walked to the sink, laid his cup in it, and went outside. I let out my breath. That seemed to go okay. But in the silence of the kitchen, I became aware of an insistent pulsing. The kitchen clock going *tick, tick, tick, tick.*

Bobbette and I had never spoken of our orphanage days. I wrote her after my Life Training weekend and told her about the memories that had surfaced.

She wrote back, "I've always felt guilty I wasn't able to protect you." It was irrational guilt; the first time we went to the orphanage, I was a baby and Bobbette was six; the next time I was four and she was ten.

Bobbette had assumed an adult role when she was very young. At age twelve, she started growing a garden so we could have nutritious food instead of the slapdash meals we were used to. I wanted to grow up to be like her—kind and responsible.

I worried about her now. She had been diagnosed with breast cancer. It was unfair; Bobbette had always emphasized nutrition and she ran half marathons. With her usual optimism, Bobbette planned to beat the cancer. She maintained her running schedule and worked even on days when she had treatments.

My mother had been single and in her mid-forties when she got pregnant with me. She referred to the man who likely was my father as "the Shanty Irisher." He came around intermittently and I liked the cigar smell of him. He was short, had large shoulders, and told the same jokes time after time, but they still made me laugh.

He disappeared for long periods, then resurfaced. At one time he'd been a successful lawyer, but his business was faltering. He liked the idea of having a child—he'd been in his mid-fifties when I was born— but had doubts about whether I was really his daughter, despite my resemblance to him. During our times together, he asked restaurant staff or the woman who cleaned his office whether I looked like him. In his last years, he became an indigent, having soaked up his talent and money in drinking.

Having daughters didn't always work into my mother's plans, especially when a new man came into her life. When dark clouds rolled in, she became physically violent. Bobbette, who was older and able to contribute to the family, didn't get sent away as much.

I'd disclosed to a couple of friends that my background had been crazy, but didn't give details. I'd wanted to appear well-adjusted. But I'd never outgrown my fear of being abandoned or punished. My insistence that I lived a contented, confident life was based on a long habit of denial.

Now I wished to live truthfully, but I remembered a long-ago discussion with my friend Dave in an ice cream shop. He'd said when someone became responsible for herself, she could lose her present life. And there was so much to love in my present life.

In the mornings, on a clear day, the Teton peaks 150 miles away glowed pink on the eastern horizon, the size of a man's thumbs. Mornings were hectic and I didn't linger watching sunrises, but when the sun set in the evening, the day's busyness generally lay behind me, so I went outside and gazed west. From my viewing spot, sunsets ranged from pretty to heartstopping. When the sky first started turning pink, clouds—wherever they were in the bowl of the sky—got pink bellies. The color would change, from purple to deep red, to flaming orange, or striped with all those shades. Foothills to the south turned an eerie magenta, and rock formations not viewable in full daylight became visible.

The sun itself would metamorphize as the day died. It would be first a pink ball, then violet, then orange, then glow in stunning red just before sinking onto the desert.

In summer, after thunderstorms, everything smelled like sagebrush. In winter, our fields turned into postcard scenes. Snow fell in huge flakes, stuck to the trees, and coated the fence railings in marshmallow. The stillness of the country after a snowfall made it seem as if the land was praying.

We lived far enough from town that our night skies held a jillion stars. When I went out on the porch at night, I'd lean my head back so far I'd be in danger of falling over. Even summer nights grew chilly, so I associated stargazing with cold cheeks and ears, in a good, extra-alive way.

On one such night, Duncan came with me to the porch.

"If I change, you'll still like me, won't you, Duncan?"

He gave me his happy doggy grin.

Years before on a cold night, I'd sought reassurance from him on the issue of livestock deaths, asking him how many I'd need to endure. I'd sensed an answer from him. There'd be many, but he'd be with me.

Splitting with George would be a different kind of death. I had a deep desire to keep our family intact. My mother and her siblings had collected many spouses. My cousin joked that the motto embroidered on our family coat-of-arms read, *You Can Never Be Married Too Many Times*. Matt and Shane would head off to college soon, but I hated the idea of Mary growing up without a dad in the home, as I had.

Still, married or single, I'd have stars. And sunsets. I'd have winter days when snow blanketed the hayfield and frosted the trees in white.

And there would be Duncan. Faithful, smart, and happy Duncan. Sticking to me like Velcro.

TWENTY-THREE

When I arrived at Mary's school for sixth-grade graduation, I saw George's car in the parking lot. I sat in my car for a minute, feeling empty and strange.

In the school cafeteria, I sat down in a vacant chair next to George. I hoped we didn't look like a couple who had split three days before.

"Mary will be receiving the Hope of America Award," I told George.

He nodded.

"Only one boy and one girl per class," I said.

Another nod.

The sixth-grade students filed in, Mary among them. I wondered if behind her calm face she might be slipping her moorings.

Mary's teacher took the mike and called Mary and a boy to the stage.

"This award is given for academic excellence and outstanding citizenship," the teacher said. Then she invited us, parents of the recipients, to come to the stage for a photo. Four proud parents and two smiling kids. I felt fraudulent.

Students from both sixth-grade classes then marched to risers on the stage and took their places. This was the sixth-grade choir. The choir sang a patriotic number and then launched into the Diana Ross hit "If We Hold On Together," from the movie *The Land Before Time*.

I'd taken Mary to see the movie about cartoon dinosaurs when she was preschool age. At that stage of her life she was so tenderhearted she'd created a scene during the part where the young dinosaur loses his mother. I'd held her on my lap and tried to comfort her, but she cried so inconsolably that people throughout the theater turned and stared.

Now, standing between a couple of her friends, Mary sang:

If we hold on together,
I know our dreams will never die.

The young voices sang in heartbreakingly sweet tones. My chest constricted and tears threatened. "Can I hold *myself* together?" I wondered.

Beside me, George wore a phlegmatic face. And Mary apparently made no connection with the words she was singing. Where had the softhearted child gone who couldn't bear to see a cartoon dinosaur parted from its mother? Replaced, it appeared, by a tall girl with bouncing curls who scarcely had a reaction to her parents' separation.

For several mornings after George had left, Duncan issued no invitations to play. I think he knew such offers would be rejected.

The breakup had come abruptly. One day we were promising to keep working on the marriage; a few days later, I found George packing. I asked him not to go. But I didn't plead.

I'd intended to call Matt and Shane and explain, but Matt arrived home for spring break earlier than expected. He came in on George collecting a last load of clothing. I returned from town to find Matt sitting on the sofa, stunned.

"I don't know what to say," I said. I put my hand on his and we cried. I felt horrible that I'd insisted on keeping our marital difficulties from the kids. Matt had been blindsided.

I called Shane and broke the news. Under the circumstances, a phone conversation didn't satisfy; I had no idea how he took it.

· · ·

"Mary," I *whispered into her sleeping ear. "I need help."*

She came to life immediately and jumped out of bed. She ran upstairs, pulled on her coveralls and a hat, and followed me to the barn.

George and I had been cutting back on the number of sheep we kept; even so, at the time of our separation, we had sixty animals on the place. Mary pitched in willingly, but I wanted her own activities, like ballet, to continue in a normal way. Yet, if a birthing ewe had trouble in the night, I had to call on Mary for help.

I'd visited Mary's teacher and tearfully explained what was going on in Mary's life. The teacher said she'd seen no changes in Mary. At a spring 4-H meeting, Mary signed up to take a large number of summer projects. After the meeting, when a friend asked me how I was getting along, I burst into tears. Mary stood nearby with a sympathetic face but had no tears of her own.

Every few days I'd ask, "How are you doing with all this?"

"Fine." She smiled.

"It's normal for kids to feel, when parents split up, that it might be their fault, or they somehow caused it. Sometimes kids feel like the bottom has fallen out."

"I don't feel that way," Mary said.

"It would be natural to feel sad."

"I don't."

A psychologist friend warned me a child sometimes tried to fill the spot of the absentee parent and became a surrogate spouse. So I took time to walk with my women friends, and before I felt entirely ready, accepted invitations from men to dinner or movies.

Chores included milking Goldie, our goat, morning and night; washing the equipment used for feeding bum lambs; treating lambs who were ill; keeping the barn clean; and feeding all the animals twice a day. It required lifting, carrying, and throwing. I felt sore all the time from crawling over fences with hay in my arms because gates didn't open. They were mired first in snow, then mud. Spring blizzards meant I sometimes had to strap on snowshoes and pull hay on a sled to the llamas and horses. Mary joined me after school as I went about my rounds, and I welcomed her help.

Because of my changed financial situation, I signed on for more freelance writing. I liked doing feature articles for the newspaper and could do most of the research and writing while Mary was at school.

I ran into an acquaintance at the grocery store.

"Are you *ill?*" she asked none too tactfully.

"No. Why?"

"Have you been to a doctor? You look like you have a serious illness."

Until that moment, I'd considered it a plus that my clothes hung on me. I might have worried over the woman's remark, but I simply had no time for it.

Bev, a friend from church, asked me one Sunday, "How are you surviving?"

I started to answer, "Fine." Instead, I told the truth. "I can't keep up with it all."

"Dennie and I will be out next Saturday. We'll bring Joni and Norm."

The next Saturday my city friends showed up in old clothes. Duncan, Mary, and I had separated lambs from their mothers and penned them in the barn. For the next few hours, the four visitors helped Mary and me put elastrator bands on all the lambs' tails, and castrate them if they were males. We weighed lambs, recorded information, and administered shots. At day's end, we were caught up.

Some days, Mary and I looked around when chores were complete, took note that our lambs were growing nicely, our barn was clean and dry, and we felt a smug satisfaction. Two women, one only pint-sized, were running the place and it was thriving.

I'd gone to dinner a few times with Will, a man who'd grown up in Chicago and had always lived in big cities before moving to Idaho. He arrived at the barn one Saturday morning just as Mary and I were preparing to vaccinate our big ram. Will looked at the 280-pound ram and asked, "How do you expect to hold him if he jumps?"

I took hold of the ram, grabbed his front leg, pulled him off balance, and put him on his back. Mary got behind the ram, propped him against her legs into a sitting position, and held him immobile while I gave the shots.

"We're showing off," Mary whispered.

"We think we're tough," I said.

Duncan, invaluable before, now had more to do. As well as accompanying me during chores and holding the sheep back while I fed them, he frequently had the role of sole helper when I needed to separate sheep. When I was holding and treating one sheep, Duncan needed to keep the rest away. If I lost hold of a sheep, he had to prevent it from returning to the others.

"Keep it in the barn, Duncan!" I'd cry. A sheep trying to return to its flock could be almost impossible to stop. But streaking back and forth like a racehorse, Duncan would stay in front of the sheep, biting the air near its head, blocking its path until it gave up. Even if a ewe bounced into the air and tried to leap over him, Duncan intercepted her.

Duncan's insistent playfulness offered my best break from busyness. His staple game was "Come Chase Me." He would dash from the house ahead of me toward the barn. After twenty feet or so, he would stop, turn, and make eye contact. Then he dropped onto his front paws, pushed his rear end into the air, wriggled, and grinned. After that, he dashed off again.

I was supposed to chase after him. He wore such a happy, expectant face, I couldn't resist. Some mornings, though, snow swirled or winds howled. Then I would mumble, "I'm not playing, Duncan."

Duncan would repeat his invitation, a couple of times if necessary, looking more winning and eager on each attempt. I wondered that he didn't notice the foul weather.

"Okay," I'd consent. "Just for a minute." Then I would cry, "I'm gonna get you, Duncan!" and run after him. He would feign surprise and tear off. On a mild, sunny morning, we would run wide circles in the backyard. On mornings when deep snow covered the yard, I wasn't willing to run after him for long.

At some point, the pursued would become the pursuer; Duncan would come speeding toward me and I would run from him. He would lunge within a foot of me, growling, but never quite manage to catch me. After a few minutes I would stop, bend over and glower at him, then begin chasing him.

It was the same game, day after day, but Duncan kept it varied. Some days he grabbed a stick and ran with it. I was supposed to try to take it from him. He would intentionally slow down so I could reach it; then we would tussle over it, both of us growling. On snowy days, Duncan stopped in flight to grab bites of snow. Some days, Duncan turned tag into hide-and-seek. After a few minutes of being chased, he would disappear from view.

"Where is Duncan?" I would ask aloud.

If Mary were present, she joined in. "I can't see him anywhere." She pointed to a black-and-white tail waving behind the edge of the haystack.

"Duncan? Where are you?" I used a singsong voice so he would know I didn't need him for work.

Suddenly, he would boil up from behind the bales and streak toward us, eyes round. I believe he thought he looked frightening. Mary and I would gasp and cower. Then he would zoom off again. He liked it if we both chased him and he had to veer and dodge more.

I found many things to worry about—the impact of divorce on the kids, a sense of personal failure, finances, writing deadlines, the workload. But at least once a day, my black-and-white friend enrolled me in a game. During those moments, that was all there was.

TWENTY-FOUR

"*So many disappointing things.*" I sat on a straw bale and stroked Duncan's ear. Duncan edged toward the bucket of goat's milk sitting near my feet.

"No," I scolded.

He lifted his ears and tried for an innocent face.

"George and me, of course. But the small things, too. Like the trip."

Ironically, George and I had been scheduled to go to a marriage workshop in California. The train tickets lay in my kitchen drawer. I loved the leisure of train travel—gazing out the window as scenery passed, the clacking of wheels, the hypnotic swaying of the train car. The tickets would go to waste now.

"Duncan, I have an idea." I picked up the milk bucket and hurried to the house to call Ronna.

"You wouldn't want to go to San Francisco by train, would you?" She couldn't, of course, because she had two small children. Stephanie, her youngest, was barely more than a toddler.

"I'll talk to Earl."

"Really?"

She called back in a few minutes. "Earl will take a few days off work and watch the kids."

I called a neighbor, who said she'd be pleased to have Mary stay at her house. Mary and the neighbor's children would do our chores and take care of Duncan. On my next phone call, I found a modestly priced motel in San Francisco within walking distance of famous spots.

On our first night in the city, Ronna and I went to a performance of the San Francisco Ballet. The next day, we walked our legs off visiting sites. We sat at a bakery in the afternoon, eating delicious bread and drinking tea. I said, "Mel says the Episcopal cathedral is beautiful and has a labyrinth."

"Let's go there next," Ronna said. "They have replicas of the Ghiberti doors. The Gates of Paradise. I learned about them in art history class."

The mammoth golden doors had sculpted panels. After gawking at them, we entered the church through a side door. A rich voice with a British accent emanated from the front pulpit.

" 'He will wipe every tear from their eyes,' " the speaker intoned.

In my present state, I only had to hear the word "tear" to get a few myself.

" 'There will be no more death or mourning or crying or pain, for the old order of things has passed away.' "

I usually avoided the writings in the book of Revelations because they were so dire, but this passage, and the voice reading it, were beautiful.

" 'I am making everything new! Write this down, for these words are trustworthy and true.' "

Ronna and I slipped past wooden pews and tall, cold pillars to a quiet corner, where we sat.

" 'I am the Alpha and the Omega, the Beginning and the End. To him who is thirsty, I will give drink without cost from the spring of the water of life.' "

I listened with belly-clenching grief. I loved the poetry in the words and the man's beautiful voice. I yearned to take comfort in them, but what I'd hoped for most—a miracle that would save my marriage—had not happened.

The small group of worshipers at the front of the church got up and filed out.

I whispered to Ronna, "I'm going to go light a candle and then walk the labyrinth."

"I'll stay here."

I found a row of candles, lighted one with care, and settled onto the kneeler. I fastened my chin on my chest and prayed that George would even now change his mind.

After a few minutes, I composed myself and walked over to the labyrinth. It was patterned after the one at Chartres, and I read the placards surrounding it. When it had become too dangerous for Christians to travel, some large churches painted labyrinths on their floors, believing that walking a labyrinth could offer the same benefits as going on a pilgrimage. One placard talked about the mathematical intricacies of the Chartres labyrinth. Another told that evidence of labyrinths had been found in almost every ancient culture, back to Neolithic times.

"Have you walked one of these before?"

I turned to see who'd spoken to me. It was a man, very handsome.

"Only once."

"Let me tell you how it works. As you walk in, toward the center, think about what it is you want to surrender. Every time you turn a corner, say what it is you are giving up. What you want to leave behind."

"Okay."

"You are traveling to your center. When you get there, take some contemplation time. Kneel if you want, or stand. Say a prayer if that's your custom."

I removed my shoes and started on my mini-pilgrimage. I knew what I wanted to give up. When I arrived at the first corner, I aimed my body in the new direction and said, "I am turning the corner on anger and fear." At every turn, I repeated the words silently.

When I got to the center, two people were there, kneeling and praying. I gazed at the stained-glass windows, my eyes traveling from one to the next.

I jumped. The man was next to me again.

"When you're done here, you go back out, to become part of the world again. As you travel out, say what it is you intend to take with you. To replace what you left behind."

I had to think on that one. What was the opposite of anger and fear? Oh. Love and faith.

"When you get to the end over there," he pointed, "and before you exit the labyrinth, take some contemplation time."

"Thank you."

I started my journey back to my regular life, repeating to myself at every corner, "I am taking on love and faith."

At the spot the man had pointed out to me, I stood in silence, observing how the light brightened the colors in the windows. I took a deep breath. My small pilgrimage was over.

But it wasn't. Because right then words came into my head, clear as a Tibetan gong. The words were, "I don't want to fix George. I want to fix you."

A gasp came out of me that I couldn't have stifled even if the nearby pews had been full.

My legs felt weak as I walked down the center aisle.

"Ronna," I whispered.

"What's wrong?" she said. "Why are you crying?"

I couldn't answer.

"Are you awfully sad?"

I shook my head, but I couldn't say anything for a while, during which time Ronna assumed I was suffering.

Finally, I could tell her.

"Was it a kind voice?"

"It wasn't a voice, exactly. But it was very kind." The words had come without a hint of judgment. They sounded full of grace.

TWENTY-FIVE

Duncan drove to town with me for my counseling appointments.
Sometimes he came in.

"If having Duncan here makes it easier, it's fine to bring him,"
Gary, my counselor, said. Being able to touch my buddy and look into
his loving eyes helped.

Once, after a hard session, I drove straight to the desert with Duncan. I parked the car and began to sob. Duncan sat close, leaning his
head into my shoulder and peering at me. He didn't hint he wanted to
get out and run the open country; he maintained his close position.
But concerned because he looked so worried, I forced myself to take
deep breaths and calm down.

I had two dogs in my childhood. The first, Lady, a Dalmatian, ran with
me as I roamed my rural neighborhood. With her at my side, I crawled
under fences and explored pastures with streams running through
them. I was preschool age but completely unsupervised. When my
mother would send me away, I missed Lady and the country.

Lady got distemper and the dogcatcher came to pick her up. Her
sad face gazing out the back window as the truck drove away stayed
with me for years, and I wrote story after forlorn story about it.

When I was nine, an aunt and uncle gave me a puppy for a birthday present. The red pup, part cocker, had a tendency to pant rhythmically, so my aunt named him Choo-Choo. I built Choo-Choo a
large doghouse from scrap lumber and put roof shingles on it. Sometimes I slept outside in the doghouse with him, and on those nights
felt safe and happy, hugging my little red dog.

I had Choo-Choo all my growing-up years, but I moved away from home as soon as I graduated from high school. Soon after that, my mother's new husband got transferred and they left Colorado. A kind neighbor fed Choo-Choo when he came around. When I learned he was running as a stray, I meant to visit him more, but I was working and taking night classes. Later, I regretted I hadn't found an apartment that would allow a dog.

In my neighborhood there had been horses, and their owners allowed me to pet, brush, and ride them. One neighbor, Mrs. Hittson, also had Shetland ponies. She flattered me by inviting me to help train them. Actually, I only sat atop them while they moved in a circle on a longe line, but I fancied I was breaking horses.

I became friends with a cow, too, whom I stopped to pet every day. The cow liked to lick my legs, maybe because she found them salty, but I interpreted it as fondness and endured her scratchy tongue and slobber. When my mother's temper raged, I found refuge with Choo-Choo, the neighbor's horses, or the old cow.

Cats came and went in my growing-up life. I had several, all of them, coincidentally, yellow. One may have been shot by a neighbor; another may have been hit by the infrequent car traveling our dirt road. Others simply vanished.

As a teenager, I bought two adorable kittens with babysitting money. I cherished them. When they were six months old, I came home one day and they were gone.

"Where are my kitties?" I asked.

My mother answered, "You didn't care about them."

"Where are they?"

"Gone," she answered with raised eyebrows.

I heard her tell a neighbor, "They drowned." I realized other cats who'd disappeared may have suffered the same fate.

It wasn't surprising I'd grow up to have a profound love for animals, and our farm allowed me to have lots of them.

I had talked with Gary about various times in my marriage when I wished I'd behaved differently. I postponed confessing the time

when I'd stood by and let George kick Duncan. When I finally told
him, I felt ashamed.

"I didn't make a move to help him."

"Why not?"

"I don't know."

"You said you were frozen. Is it possible you actually were?"

"Of course not!"

"What if at that moment you weren't an adult watching a dog get
kicked?"

"Who was I?"

"A child who knew to stay quiet because if she didn't, things
might get worse."

"Can I blame my failure on things that happened decades ago?
Don't I need to take responsibility for myself?"

"What do you think?"

"Yes!"

"How will you do that?"

I stared at the carpet a long time, my hand on Duncan's head.
Then I took a stab. "I'll heal."

TWENTY-SIX

Undergoing counseling with a professional allowed me to delve into my big issues. But milking a goat morning and evening gave me the chance to sort out day-to-day dilemmas.

I didn't actually talk things over with Goldie, our crossbred Saanen, because she didn't say anything. That was the advantage; I orchestrated the entire conversation. If I desired a response, I made one up on her behalf. I pretended that she chuckled at something funny I said, or praised me when I spoke a deep truth.

If I didn't want a response, none was forthcoming. I could tell her my private worries and she kept chewing her grain. She did not advise or try to solve things for me. She didn't give unwanted sympathy, or withhold sympathy I craved. I interpreted her chomping to signify whatever I desired.

Besides that, listening to milk pinging rhythmically against a bucket made me heavily philosophical. Though I didn't write poetry, I recognized there was something lyrical about grass and grain going in a creature's front end and coming out the other as foamy white milk.

I didn't talk only to Goldie during milking. Duncan, Lala, and Aurora sat in a row near the milking stand, confident that when milking was done, they could polish the milking stand with their tongues. Sometimes I directed my remarks to them, along with lacteal squirts.

Yet, pleasant as my morning and evening sessions were, having Goldie created two problems for me. The first was, it tied me to a schedule. Sometimes, after teaching at night or enjoying an evening in town, I had to come home, pull on coveralls, and go milk Goldie, whose bag would be bursting. The only light in the barn was a bulb hanging from a wire.

I seldom wanted to sleep in because I liked early morning, but on those few occasions when I was tempted to, it wasn't a possibility. Goldie needed to be milked. After school let out in June, Mary took over milking because she showed Goldie in 4-H. Still, Mary and I had to come early home from social events so Mary could milk.

The other problem got worse in summer—what to do with the copious amount of milk? When Goldie kidded that summer, she gave birth to two beautiful does, who Mary named Athena and Aphrodite. Even with feeding her two kids, Goldie had a quantity of milk to share. We had six bum lambs to raise—triplets or quads we had taken from their mothers. Mary let Goldie's kids eat first, then milked the excess into a bucket, which I gave to our bums. The bums thrived.

When the lambs reached a certain weight, we weaned them and put them on free choice grain and hay. Mary began to give the extra milk to the two piglets she was raising for 4-H. A hog expert warned Mary that her hogs would get too fat, but the piglets looked beautiful and sleek to us.

We gave milk to neighbors who were raising bum lambs. Still, we had leftover milk. One of our 4-H mothers started coming twice a week to pick up milk. I told her if she planned to use it for human consumption, I couldn't know. I think she was making cheese, but we avoided talking about it. Mary did not milk "clean," which involved sanitizing the teats, milking on a cement floor, and disinfecting buckets. We washed our buckets in hot soapy water and strove for cleanliness, but we didn't meet dairy standards.

We still had leftover milk.

Mary's longtime 4-H friend, Gene, said he wanted to start feeding milk to his hog.

At the 4-H fair, Gene and Mary won Champion and Reserve

Champion with their milk-fed hogs. The hogs' fat layer, tested by an ultrasound machine, showed both animals were nicely lean.

With the local fair over, we had leftover milk again. Mary and Gene each had a pig for the state fair, but those two animals, even eating like hogs, couldn't keep up with Goldie. Containers crammed every inch of freezer space and bottles lined up in our refrigerator. Throwing away rich, nutritious milk seemed wicked.

Matt, home for the summer, loved to cook.

I asked him, "What if we made cheese?"

"Hmm. Goat cheese," he said. "It's expensive in the stores."

"If we made it now, it could age through the fall and we could send it in November for Christmas presents."

Matt came home from the library with an armload of books on cheese making. I could see that Matt's approach would be different from mine. The book I read said cheese making was fun and simple, but Matt found a different message—cheese making required scientific exactness.

I wanted to jump into a large cheese-making effort, but Matt said we must work into it slowly. He considered that as beginners, we might fail. I, on the other hand, imagined urban friends and relatives exclaiming over cheese produced from our own milk.

We cooked up a batch of milk with rennet and followed the simple steps of cooking and draining. Matt placed ovals of gleaming white cheese in the basement and weighted them with bricks to act as presses.

The next day, I caught Duncan easing down the stairway.

"Duncan. Where are you going?"

He looked up, sheepish.

"You don't need to check the progress of the cheese."

He sidled up the stairs, tail glued to his backside. He had too much conscience to be a good sneak thief, but even so, over the next few days I caught him tiptoeing toward the stairway when he thought no one was watching.

After a few days more, we sampled the cheese. Good flavor. Acceptable texture. Nice appearance. I saw no reason not to jump into making a big batch.

Matt said, "We don't have anything large enough to hold all the milk we've stored."

"I'll go find something," I said.

At a farm store, I bought a galvanized tub that covered all four burners on the stove. We dumped our abundance of milk into it for pasteurizing.

Matt hovered over the stove reading a book and drawing circles in the milk with a wooden spoon. He stirred and stirred and stirred for an hour, watching the milk's temperature climb by degrees. Mary came in the house and sniffed. "What smells?"

A scorched smell had invaded the kitchen. No question, it was burning. Matt stirred faster. After two hours, the milk reached the proper temperature and we set it aside to cool. The kitchen stank.

We tasted the milk. Bad.

I'd read somewhere that slices of dried bread could remove a scorched flavor. I covered the top of the milk with bread. After letting the bread soak, I gave it to Duncan. He sniffed it and blinked. Gracie loved bread, so I gave her some. She backed up from her bowl and frowned.

We tried to camouflage the burned flavor with salt. It didn't help. Two of us carried the tub to the pig, who, contrary to anything I'd ever seen, walked away from it.

I hosed out the bucket so it could go to an animal pen, but noticed it had cracked from being on the stove. We trashed it.

We still had cheese from our first batch. I retrieved one from the basement to make sandwiches. A film of green mold covered it.

"That's natural," I told Matt. "Cut into it." It was green throughout.

We threw away that batch and made another, a small one. It molded more quickly.

"Your house stinks," an honest 4-H'er observed.

"Sterilization is our problem," Matt theorized. "We'll be cleaner."

He washed the cooking pans, spoons, and presses in Clorox. The next batch tasted like bleach. I thought I could overlook the flavor, and maybe friends and relatives could, too, but that cheese also molded.

We decided to try something simpler. Matt made soft cheeses— cottage cheese, ricotta, and feta. They turned out delicious. The ricotta went into Monday night lasagna, and we agreed it was the best lasagna we'd ever tasted. We had much ricotta to use, so Wednesday night dinner was lasagna, too, and so was Friday's. By then, we'd stopped exclaiming over it.

Matt searched recipe books and found a recipe for tiramisu that used ricotta. The other ingredients were egg bread, coffee, shaved chocolate, heavy cream, and an expensive liqueur.

We served it to guests. "This is a million-dollar dessert," one commented. I'd calculated it cost seventy dollars.

Fall was coming. We had to dry up Goldie. We cut her grain to a minimum and didn't empty her udder when we milked. She kept milking profusely.

One day when we were driving on I-15, Matt pointed out a peaceful scene of goats grazing happily.

"Maybe it's a dairy," Mary said.

I turned at the next exit and backtracked to the farm. It was indeed a dairy, run by a couple who prized their goats. We watched them bring their goats in from the pasture and hook them to automatic milkers.

I explained about Goldie.

"What a problem to have. A goat that milks too heavily," the woman said.

We looked at each other. Goldie had a wonderful personality and we appreciated her as an outstanding producer, but all that milk made a problem for us.

We sold Goldie to the dairy. When we delivered her, the woman looked at Goldie's udder and said, "Wow! Look at that." We felt proud our goat had impressed a professional dairyman.

One morning I found Athena, Mary's beautiful doe, dead in the barn. I looked around for the cause. She had pulled down a ski pole and eaten the basket off it.

We bred Aphrodite, confident it would take her a couple of years before she started milking as heavily as her mother had.

I didn't miss the tyrannizing routine of milking. But I did miss the conversation.

TWENTY-SEVEN

One thing caused Duncan as much distress as approaching storms. That was suitcases. Just as storms made him jittery hours before any cloud appeared, an upcoming departure turned Duncan into a sad sack days before the first suitcase came out.

When Duncan sensed Matt and Shane would be returning to college, he began to drag, ears at half-mast. Their departures had become a fact of life, but Duncan couldn't get okay about it.

It was August. I was trying to enjoy my morning tea and toast, but flies buzzed my head and dove at my food. Flies swarming me as I did chores annoyed me plenty, but when they intruded on my breakfast, they'd flown over the line. I went upstairs to my computer and typed a proclamation of war. I would enlist the kids in the battle.

The proclamation read:

Citizens of Our Farm,

In every century and every country, young men and women have been called upon to protect their homes from intruders.

At this critical time (August), flying invaders threaten us. Can you be counted on to help repel them? Will loyalty propel you to outrage, outrage to action?

On this day, I issue weapons. A flyswatter for each. Sweep the enemy out of the air! Give no quarter! Take no prisoners!

Realizing that armies move on their stomachs, I pledge to treat the winning fly slayer to pizza at his or her favorite restaurant.

Please record your kills on the chart below. We will observe the honor system.

May you show unflagging determination in defense of your home.

The kids jumped into the campaign. I bought swatters in assorted colors, but it was design that interested my troops. Shane thought the traditional style of woven fabric with a wire handle had stood the test of time. Matt and Mary liked plastic ones with translucent handles.

The male soldiers experimented with applying principles of physics to their swings. Mary practiced a martial arts position she called Fly Chi. Flies on windowsills, furniture, and in the air came under attack. Bodies collected on the floor. I swept them up.

Duncan happily joined the effort. While kids were swatting, he leaped at passing flies, jaws clicking. We weren't able to enter him in the competition, though, because we couldn't record his kills. They disappeared down his throat.

Now a different threat to my peace and quiet surfaced. The corps of dedicated fly killers hardly took a break. Once at dinner, as I was putting a forkful of casserole into my mouth, pain suddenly stung my shoulder. Mary, gripping her weapon said, "Sorry. Getting a fly."

I hoped I might be able to give up my summer mantra, "Shut the door, shut the door, shut the door," because the fly killers would want the fly population to diminish. Instead, they opened the door more to invite in targets.

Shane's summer job kept him at work until 10 P.M., so he fell behind. Matt and Mary paced the kitchen in the afternoons, swatters ready. On an especially lethal day, Matt's body count rose to forty-five.

Fly puns accumulated in a growing stockpile. Among the soldiers, a sense of purpose and esprit de corps formed.

But a day came when Duncan refused to join in with the others. He slunk behind the sofa and stared glumly at the floor. Somehow he knew school would be starting soon.

"Duncan, they'll be back," I told him.

On a hot afternoon, Duncan and I watched Shane load his car. We stood on the porch as he drove out our sagebrush-lined driveway and pointed his car toward faraway Texas. We didn't move, watching the car shrink until it was a speck.

A week later, Mary, with gleaming hair and new jeans, boarded the bus for junior high.

Matt, the bronze-star fly killer, and I dined on pizza at a local restaurant. He talked about his upcoming year.

"Next summer I'm going to try for a university research position," he said. Midway through the sentence, his hand shot up and grabbed a fly. He squished it in his hand. "I'm quick," he observed.

The morning I drove him back to Salt Lake City felt chilly. I helped Matt unload his things and said a quick good-bye. Duncan and I said hardly a word on the way home.

The next morning, I drank my tea in quiet. No young men getting ready for work. No Mary chattering about her 4-H animals. A fly circled the table, but it didn't land.

Summer, like childhood, had played a short run. Autumn had stolen in before I'd had my fill of picnics and mountain getaways. At night, the sun turned itself off before I was ready to come inside. My children had grown so tall they had to be kissed good-bye from a stepladder.

I said to Duncan. "To everything there is a season."

His head hung limply on his neck.

"Me, too, buddy." I found no comfort in the words. I was looking over my shoulder and yearning for summer, even if it came with flies.

TWENTY-EIGHT

"Kin ya see 'em there?" Rob, *the Scot, pointed at the small screen attached* to his ultrasound equipment.

"Um, yeah." I thought it polite to say yes, though I couldn't see the lamb fetuses. All I saw was murky haze. I saw movement in the murkiness, but no tiny lambs. Rob, who lived in Oregon, traveled the region in the fall, visiting sheep outfits. He had been checking our pregnant ewes for years, but still I wasn't able to see lambs in utero.

Jake, a ten-year-old 4-H kid, walked on his knees to the screen and touched his finger to it.

"Here's one, and here's two."

"D' ya see the third?"

Jake stared. "Here!" He grinned and raised his fist. Duncan, staring at the screen, wagged. He probably saw them, too. Everyone could, except me.

Jake sat back down on the barn's dirt floor. He had offered to record information about our ewes because Mary and I were busy moving and holding them. Jake had brought over his one Suffolk ewe for an ultrasound and learned she was carrying twins.

Jake recorded the ear tag numbers of our ewes and how many lambs each was carrying. After Rob and the 4-H'ers left, Mary, Duncan, and I would sort the ewes into separate pens consisting of mothers of twins, triplets, and quads, and start them on separate feeding programs. It didn't make economic sense to overfeed ewes that were carrying twins, and besides, if the ewes got too fat, that could contribute to lambing problems. On the other hand, we would shovel feed to mothers of quads, especially during their last month of gestation, so the lambs would be born strong. If any ewes showed up barren we wouldn't keep them; we'd send them to the local sheep sale.

Ultrasounding helped us in another way. The experienced Rob could predict to the day when a ewe would lamb. He'd squint at the screen, study the images of the lambs, and announce, "Eighty-six days!" meaning the ewe was eighty-six days into her five-month gestation. Particularly with triplets and quads, that information made us extra vigilant as the ewe's lambing date approached, so we could get lambs suckled and under heat lamps quickly.

Mary and I sent a ewe on her way and I brought over another. Mary braced it from the front and Rob pushed the probe through the wool to get to the animal's skin. The ewe was Cassiopeia, one of Mary's favorites. Mary leaned way over to glimpse the screen.

"Good! Quads!"

Jacob marked a "Q" beside Cassiopeia's number.

"Where do you see them?" I mumbled to Mary.

She gave me an odd look. "See there on the left? There's one, then look over to the right a little. See?"

Rob told Bryce, a teenage boy, to come hold the ewe. I moved around to gaze at the screen. Rob aimed my head. "Rrright there! Surely you can see 'em!"

"Uh, sort of."

"There's no sort of! Ya see 'em or ya don't."

I shrugged apologetically. Rob adjusted my head, a bit roughly.

And then, like the moment when you spy a bird's nest hidden among branches, or a distant hawk circling, I saw them. I saw first a spine and ribs, then a heart, contracting and expanding. I saw another spine, and another. The overall picture remained murky, but I saw them—the incipient lambs.

"Kin ya count four?"

"Here's one. Here's another. And here—" I'd lost the fourth. "Oh! Here."

A minute later, feeling self-satisfied, I walked to the house to draw a bucket of warm water for Rob. This year, I had enjoyed fall. The pearly everlasting that grew in our yard kept blooming through September. Matt, Mary, and I had gathered chokecherries in the foothills and I'd made syrup and Matt had made chokecherry ice cream.

Self-help books, when discussing perception, say we often fail to see what is right before us. They mention as an example the popular painting of paint horses. In that picture, the horses blend into rocks of variegated colors. A person can stare and stare but see only rocks, no horses. Finally, the viewer's eye relaxes, or the brain starts to perceive in a different way, or the light in the room shifts, and the horses become visible and the person wonders how he missed them before.

Heading back to the barn, swinging a bucket of warm water, I couldn't resist doing a metaphor myself. I had months of counseling behind me now. I, who'd lived in terror of the other shoe falling, had watched the shoe fall with a thud. Yet, whatever I'd feared would happen (had I thought I'd die?) had not.

Maybe an ultrasound image didn't lend itself to metaphor like the paint horse picture did. Or maybe it made a better one, because when the picture finally came into focus for me, I saw new life.

TWENTY-NINE

"*Don't let me get a puppy.*" *I steered the car around a curve on the foothills* road leading to our friends' sheep ranch. Steve and Tami nearly always had new pups around.

"I promise," Mary said.

A half hour later, Mary and I sat on hay bales, each cuddling a pup.

"I really like this one." Mary held an almost all-white Border collie. "Look how affectionate she is."

"You're supposed to prevent me from taking a puppy home."

"But you didn't say I couldn't." She tucked the pup under her neck. I tried for a grimace.

"It's almost my birthday. This pup could be my present."

I liked the rationale.

For Mary's fourteenth birthday, Mel and Jim invited us to dinner and generously included Mary's puppy, now named Mimi. Mary ended up holding Mimi all through dinner because the pup whined with agony whenever Mary put her in the kennel.

As she grew, Mimi showed strong herding ability but not much interest. Instead, she kept careful watch on people, waiting for one to sit down so she could crawl onto a lap. This worked out for the best because Duncan had no intention of sharing his herding work.

Mimi wouldn't go up or down stairs, and she disliked riding in vehicles. She never overcame her fear of stairs, but she did learn to tolerate an occasional ride in the truck when she figured out that rides offered the potential of sitting on someone's lap.

"Let's set up the barn a different way." Mary, smudged and dirty, rested a wooden panel against her legs.

"Okay. Unless it requires more work." Since the day before, Mary and I had been preparing for lambing. We'd collected panels to use for constructing lambing jugs, spread lime on the barn floor to make it sanitary, and stacked straw bales against the barn walls to block drafts. Earlier in the week, I'd hired a man to shovel and haul away manure and he'd scraped the barn to bare ground.

Usually, we constructed jugs in a line along one wall. But Mary said, "If we put all the jugs together, we can use fewer panels. With heat lamps hanging close together, that section will stay warmer."

"Lead the way." I picked up the panel I was holding. "Move, Duncan."

Mary directed and I helped carry panels and tie them together with baling twine. I didn't make sense of what we were constructing until suddenly, I saw it. Jugs were clustered for warmth, and we wouldn't have to carry water and feed as far.

"Nice arrangement, Mary."

We ran extension cords from the house and strung a wire above the jugs for hanging heat lamps.

I brought the ladder over. "Move, Duncan."

Mary climbed the ladder and tied the heat lamps in place, and checked to make sure they were working.

A rule of thumb said we should have one jug for every four ewes, but we always built more than the suggested ratio. Hard experience had taught us that constructing jugs in the middle of the night to make room for new mothers was too stressful.

"Let's take these long panels and make a Presidential Jug for mothers who have quads," Mary said.

For one side of the jug, we used a metal sorting panel that had a walk-through gate. Whoever delivered water and hay to the Presidential Jug wouldn't have to crawl over panels.

I walked around the yard and gathered up watering buckets. Duncan picked up a bucket by the handle and dragged it along the ground, trying to get me to chase him. "Not now, Duncan."

On a table in a corner of the barn, Mary lined up our vet supplies—obstetrical gloves, iodine, a triangular-shaped device we inserted in a ewe in case of uterine prolapse, the scale for weighing lambs, and wound ointment.

I looked around. "Can it be, we're all ready?" I'd checked ewes earlier in the week and several were making milk bags.

"I love it when the lambs start coming." Mary had favorite ewes, and she looked forward to seeing their babies. She didn't just help with the outdoor work; she had taken over a task I disliked. She kept the records required by our purebred association. She had a head of thick, curly hair, and she smiled a lot. She made jokes that were clever beyond her age. She loved ballet, and I enjoyed watching her rehearse for performances. Periodically, I'd ask how she was doing with the divorce.

"I'm a lot better now," I told her. "If you need a turn—"

"At what?"

"Falling apart?"

She looked like I had spoken in a foreign tongue. "No-o-o."

Friends of mine who worked at the junior high told me Mary had started to run with questionable friends. But that Sunday we stood there as a team, proud of our efforts.

"Let's reward ourselves by going to town for a hamburger." Mary put on her best smile.

"We could do that."

At the fast food place, as we unwrapped our sandwiches, I said, "It doesn't seem to me that you do much with Lara anymore."

"She's boring."

"In what way?"

"She's such a conformist."

"How about Kelly?"

"Boring." So were Sarah and Mandy and Melissa. I liked those girls very much, and knew them to be well supervised.

"Who do you like nowadays?"

"Different girls."

"Do they have names?"

Mary's mouth pulled into a lipless line. She turned to the window and glared out at the parking lot. Our congenial mood had evaporated.

When I heard the school bus the next afternoon, I went to the driveway and hollered to Mary, "Put on your coveralls and come out."

She arrived a moment later.

"We're off to a grand start. Look!"

I pointed to our first ewe who had lambed and her small but healthy triplets.

"Is this Dolley Madison?" Mary asked.

"Yes."

Dolley Madison, the prettiest of our young sheep, was not yet twelve months old.

"Dolley Madison! Good for you!" Mary said.

We'd been selecting for early puberty and nearly all of our ewe lambs gave birth to twins. But triplets from a first-time lamber were even better. If we didn't keep Dolley's two female lambs, we could sell them for a good price. We would watch the third lamb, a male, to see how fast he grew, because he was a likely ram candidate.

"Why have you got Dolley tied up?" Mary asked.

"She's skittish. She acts scared of the lambs."

Mary, the record keeper, went to the jug. She gave Dolley Madison a stern look. "You're from the Topaz line. You can't be a bad mother." She reached over to touch Dolley. Dolley jerked her head and stared at Mary with wild eyes.

"What's wrong with her?"

"She's acting like she hasn't got good sense." We hadn't handled this sheep except for inoculations since it was a lamb, but that was true of many of our ewe lambs and usually they calmed down in the jugs and didn't mind being handled. For most of them, having lambs put them in a deliriously good mood.

"You should have seen how much trouble I had getting her in. She acted berserk and wouldn't follow her lambs. I had to call Duncan to help." I'd hoped when Duncan arrived it might scare Dolley into taking an interest in her lambs. Instead, she'd only acted crazier and fled to a distant corner of the corral. The only way I could get her into a jug was by having Duncan chase her in. Once she was trapped, I'd made a rope halter, wrestled it onto her head, and tied her to a floor joist so she couldn't jump out.

"I gathered up the lambs and tried to coax her into cleaning them up, but she stared at them like she's terrified. I dried them off myself."

"Have the lambs nursed?" Mary asked.

"No, I tried to hold them on, but she was too jumpy. I couldn't do it by myself."

Mary stepped over a panel and took a firm hold on Dolley Madison. The ewe flung her body and tried to get free. "Wow! She's strong," Mary said.

"Maybe once she nurses them, she'll decide it's all right."

"Don't be scared," Mary said kindly, barely hanging on. Mary, a strong, young animal herself, looked outmatched.

One by one, I managed to hold each lamb on a teat and give it a turn suckling.

"They're eager lambs," I said. If a lamb wasn't enterprising, getting it to nurse could be a problem. But these lambs were smarter than their loony mother; they stubbornly held on to a teat and guzzled colostrum even as the ewe tried to escape.

"She's got a good bag for a young ewe," Mary said. We would take one lamb off and raise it ourselves, but it would be best if Dolley Madison raised the other two.

Mary looked exhausted from the wrestling match. "Are we done?"

"Finally. Let's go eat. We'll do her once more before bedtime."

"Oh boy."

"I'll leave her tied up. I don't think she can hurt the lambs."

"She looks like she'd stomp them if she could."

"Maybe she's deranged?" I didn't know if sheep could be crazy, but it happened in horses and dogs and certainly people.

"We don't allow snotty ewes around here," Mary threatened Dolley as we left the barn.

After supper, I drove Mary to her dance class. I came home, did chores, and checked sheep udders. Three ewes had warm bags, which meant the bags had filled. The ewes' voices had become lower, too, in rehearsal for the deep chuckle they would use to talk to their newborn lambs.

At bedtime, Mary and I started to force Dolley Madison into suckling her lambs. But her bag was empty, and it seemed like a lot of effort with little payoff.

"I'll thaw some colostrum and give each of the lambs a bottle," I told Mary.

Not every lamb took to bottles. Some preferred their mother's colostrum and teats and refused the strange nipples we offered. But Dolley's lambs each drank a couple of ounces. Good thing, because the night ahead was going to be cold, and they'd need the energy.

I set my alarm for 1 A.M., which was only a couple of hours away, and fell asleep. When the alarm went off, I pulled on coveralls and boots and headed for the barn.

The light from Dolley Madison's heat lamp, along with my headlamp, allowed me to see that in one corner, a ewe was cleaning up newborns. I eased over, and when I got close, saw it was Tulip, a three-year-old. She hardly looked up when I approached.

"Well, look at you. Another set of triplets." Tulip looked up then, pleased, I thought.

"Maybe I can help you clean them up and make sure they get nursed."

Duncan sat at the barn entrance, awaiting an invitation to come in.

"Stay there," I told him.

His ears hung.

Not worrying about a strategy for getting Tulip to a jug, I gathered all three lambs in my arms and walked off at a normal pace. Tulip followed, blatting with concern.

I enclosed the new family in a jug and went to the house for towels. Two of the lambs, I'd noticed, had cold ears.

A few minutes later, I was sitting in the straw rubbing sweet-faced lambs with a towel. Two heat lamps cast a cozy light and my insulated coveralls and a woolen headband protected me from the cold. Our lambing year had gotten off to a great start.

"Let's get colostrum in their bellies," I suggested to Tulip. I picked up a lamb and tried to help it find the teat. Tulip, good mother that she was, thrust her hips forward to assist the lamb. In the dim light it was hard to see if the lamb was getting anything. I couldn't hear swallowing. I put my finger in the lamb's mouth. Its tongue was cold.

The lambs had gotten hypothermic and simply wouldn't nurse. The only remedy was to warm them so the sucking reflex would return.

"I hate to do this," I told Tulip. "I'm going to have to take these guys in the house."

She was bent over two of the lambs, happily licking them. I didn't have the heart to take all three, so I left her the largest and presumably heartiest, and carried the other two to the house. I put a heating pad at the bottom of a cardboard box, covered it with newspapers, and put the lambs in the box. They weren't in crisis yet but were acting dumpy—making little effort to stand and hardly blatting at all.

"You're the babysitter," I told Duncan.

He'd already assumed that job. He sat next to the box, his head hanging over it, giving the lambs occasional licks. I returned to the barn and tried to get the largest lamb to suckle. He had no interest in the teat and his neck was getting limp. It didn't take long for lambs to sink into crisis when temperatures were in the zero range and before they'd had colostrum. After they'd had colostrum, they were nearly indestructible.

I took Tulip's big lamb to the house and deposited him with his siblings.

Fortunately, by then, the smallest of the lambs had perked up.

"Didn't take you long." I felt the lamb's mouth. It seemed normal. I'd return it to Tulip, who had blatted in alarm when I took away the last of her lambs.

Back at the barn, the smallest lamb went after the teat with vigor. Tulip talked encouragement to him. A mother like Tulip would offer a lot of assistance by pushing the lamb toward her bag and standing rigid while the lamb searched for the teat, but I stayed long enough to make sure he got a few swallows.

I'd put Tulip in a jug two away from Dolley Madison. I wondered if I should have put her next door to Dolley, so Dolley could take note of what good mothering looked like. Every time I passed Dolley Madison, her eyes rolled with a feral look. I wasn't going to attempt to nurse her lambs again in the night; it would be easier to give them bottles.

The lambs warming in the house looked better by the time I returned, but when I felt their mouths, they were still cool.

I put water in the microwave to heat. "I'm having tea, Duncan. What would you care for?"

He walked to the pantry and gazed at the top shelf.

"Oatmeal? Is that what you're looking at?"

Duncan and Gracie both loved bowls of warm oatmeal on a cold night. I made a bowl for Duncan, then carried one to Gracie, who was curled up asleep in a feeder in the drop pen.

"Gracie," I whispered. I didn't want to disturb the ewes, who were scattered around the pen sleeping or chewing their cuds. If they thought I'd shown up to feed them, they would set up a racket.

Gracie bounded over to me. Her face lit up when she saw what I'd brought.

I returned Tulip's other two lambs to her. It was close to 3 A.M. Now, from another corner of the barn, I heard another ewe chuckling. I went back to the house for my headlamp.

There were two lambs on the ground when I got back. Eleanor Roosevelt, another yearling, was licking the lambs with so much vigor it looked like she'd take the hide off them.

"Nice lambs, Eleanor." Eleanor was herself a triplet. We knew her well because she'd been adorable as a lamb and managed to get a lot of extra attention. Eleanor panicked when I picked up her lambs, and it took several tries to get her to a jug. By then, another water bag was hanging from her rear end. She, too, was having triplets.

"Good job!" I told her. I put her in the jug between Tulip and Dolley Madison.

On my next trip to the house, I warmed bottles for Dolley's lambs, who were huddled together for warmth and had stopped approaching their mother to try to nurse.

For the next hour, I shuttled lambs that needed warming between the house and their mothers. Sometimes when I returned to the house, Duncan would meet me with a concerned look. A formerly dumpy lamb would have jumped out of the box and be running around the kitchen. For me, the relief of seeing a lamb doing better made up for the mess.

There was no point in going to bed now. In a couple of hours, it would be daylight and I could carry hay and water to everyone. My eyes felt like they had weights on them and my body ached, but it had been a banner night. I went back to the barn to check on everyone.

Dolley Madison's bag looked full and tight, and probably felt uncomfortable. I wasn't going to try to nurse her lambs, but colostrum was liquid gold and I hated to see it go to waste. If I could pin Dolley to the wall, I could milk her out.

When I stepped into her jug, she reared up on her hind legs.

"Quit, you fool! I'm just going to milk you."

She jerked away from me, almost stepping on a sleeping lamb.

"Be careful!" I ordered.

I couldn't use the wall for a barrier unless I untied her from the floor joist. I did that, and retied her to a panel. Then I put an arm under her neck and pushed her flat against the barn wall. With my other hand, I touched her bag.

She jumped out of her skin. She hurled herself against me and knocked me over. I took hold of her again. She probably didn't weigh much more than I did, but she had astonishing strength. When I

touched her bag again, she exploded. The panel I'd tied her to started
to wobble. Dolley's lambs jumped as the pen started to collapse. Fortunately, no panel hit them, but the jug that housed Eleanor started to
slip, too.

I tried to hold Dolley against the wall to stop the domino effect of
falling panels. But she thrashed harder and pulled over the panel
joining her jug to Eleanor Roosevelt's. Panels were falling everywhere,
and now Tulip's jug started to collapse.

All the panels Mary and I had constructed fell. It was a wonder
no lamb got killed or hurt. Tulip and Eleanor Roosevelt stampeded
in fright. Nine newborn lambs blatted in terror, ran in circles, got
lost, and mixed together.

Crazy Dolley Madison, still tied to a panel, tore to the end of the
barn. If she hadn't been wearing the panel, she would have outrun
me all night and the next day. As it was, I was able to grab an end of
the panel and work my way to her, then grab her by the neck.

From the door, Duncan yipped.

"Outside!" With everyone so scared already, I didn't need a dog
making things worse.

I got hold of Dolley by the wool on either side of her neck.

"You devil!" I pushed her against the wall. I pinned her side with
my knee and pushed my fists against her throat. Her eyes bulged in
fright and she became rigid.

"You lunatic!" My fists sunk deeper into her wool. She started to
make a strangling noise. "Go ahead, choke!" My strength amazed me.
With my bare hands, I could kill her.

I felt something touch my thigh. I glanced down, and Duncan
had placed a paw on my leg. He strained his nose toward my face. His
expression said, "Don't."

I let go of Dolley. She slumped against the wall, coughing. I covered
my eyes. I couldn't look at the damage in the barn and didn't want to
see Dolley, choking and cowering.

After a minute, I tugged Dolley back to the floor joist and tied her
securely. One by one, I rebuilt the jugs. Then I set about catching lambs

and their mothers. Eleanor Roosevelt and Tulip were too frightened to return to a jug. But after I'd caught all the lambs and had them mostly sorted and in jugs, the ewes cautiously came around.

I pushed Tulip into her jug and tied the panel shut. She sniffed all her lambs. She sniffed one several times and frowned at me.

"Okay," I said, "let me see if she belongs to Eleanor." Eleanor happily claimed the lamb, and I found Tulip's baby among Eleanor's.

I went back to the house and sat on the icy porch step stroking Duncan and staring at the cold stars, thinking, as Wordsworth said, "Thoughts that do often lie too deep for tears." I'd always seen myself as kind. Sure, I was sleep deprived, physically exhausted, and numb from the cold. And Dolley Madison could have hurt or killed baby lambs. But just because she'd acted psychotic, did that give me license to behave the same? How would the scene have played out if Duncan hadn't been there?

We had started our lambing year with a 300 percent lamb crop. I should have felt exultant. Instead, I felt sad.

The next morning, I made Dolley Madison's lambs into bums. I thawed goat's milk and taught the lambs to use the automatic feeder, a bucket with several nipples. The lambs could help themselves to milk whenever they wanted and would grow almost as well as lambs raised by their mothers.

I took one lamb from Eleanor Roosevelt and tried it on the feeder. It stoutly refused to try the artificial nipples. I tried another of her lambs and it latched on and guzzled. That one would be raised as a bum. Eleanor cried from her jug all day, telling her lamb in the orphan pen she missed it.

I turned Dolley Madison out with the meat wethers. I wasn't going to risk having her near the lambing barn. She flew to the pasture like a maniac, ran around in the field like she'd never seen it before, and it took her an hour to settle down.

The rest of the week went easier. Ewes lambed mostly in the daytime and without difficulty. I got naps between barn checks. Sunshine in the daytime warmed things, and at night the lambs and their mothers stayed snug under heat lamps.

On the following weekend, Mary pulled Dolley Madison's papers from our purebred file and tore them up.

"Don't bother doing any paperwork on her lambs, either," I told Mary. "We'll sell them as meat lambs."

"But the lambs are gentle. We could give them a chance."

"We don't want to risk that heredity showing up anywhere."

On Monday, Duncan and I had a terrible time getting Dolley Madison loaded into the trailer. But then I drove her to the livestock auction. I'd thought we'd get almost nothing for her, assuming buyers would notice she'd already lambed and wouldn't be producing anything until the next year, and she'd sell for slaughter. But when I picked up the check the next day, I was surprised to see she'd sold for a decent price. Not what she would have brought as a purebred, but still, for good money.

"I feel guilty," I told Mary. "Somebody believes they got a good ewe."

"It was her looks that sold her," Mary said. She added optimistically, "Maybe she'll do better on her second lambing."

To me, it seemed more likely someone might slit her throat or bludgeon her to death. My concern wasn't for the ewe. I felt for a beleaguered shepherd who, on a night of little sleep and low patience, might discover a side to him or herself best left unrevealed.

THIRTY
·····················

"That's the first time I've seen you mad," Ronna said.

"What an awful, awful person." I watched an old man disappearing from view. Ronna and I had encountered the grouch as we walked the Idaho Falls Greenbelt. I'd moved Duncan off the sidewalk, out of the man's way, but the guy had veered out of his way to give Duncan a kick. The impact had rolled over the astonished Duncan.

"You cussed out that guy."

"What'd I say?"

"I don't know. It happened so fast."

I'd started out politely enough. I'd caught up with the old man and told him he'd been unkind. He yelled at me that if he had a chance, he'd kick the dog again. After that, it became a blur.

"You went at him with your fists balled," Ronna said.

"Wow. I wished I'd hit him."

"He backed up too fast."

The money, time, and grief I'd spent in counseling had been worth it.

"Ain't nobody gonna kick my dawg around."

Other family members felt the same.

I walked into the house and inhaled cooking smells. Matt and Shane sat at the table, dishing meat onto their plates.

"Pot roast? But there's a whiff of bacon, too."

"We cooked a pound of bacon and ate it before we made the roast."

Matt and Shane, home for the summer, had adopted an anabolic diet and weight-lifting regimen. The diet encouraged huge amounts of protein and fat. The diet was purported to have a steroidlike effect on the body, yet was completely natural, if eating like a lion could be considered natural.

Shane had put on twenty pounds of muscle during the previous semester and another twenty since he'd been home. He talked up the program wherever he went, and one convert he made was his brother. Matt, formerly a long-distance runner and now a cyclist, had always been slim, though he had good shoulders and muscular legs. Now he resembled a football player. Shane himself had turned into a giant. He consumed huge quantities of meat and eggs and carried a package of cheese wherever he went. He tried to convert me, but I lacked any desire to bulk up.

On top of the stove, bratwursts, omelets, and pork chops always were cooking. The house smelled like a restaurant. Pastas and breads, which had been a staple of our life, had disappeared.

"I saw your son the other day," a high school coach told me. "Why didn't I have him in football?"

"He didn't look like this in high school," I said.

It was at this time, when no one, including his family, was used to Shane being a behemoth, that he was called on to come to Duncan's aid.

Some kids in our 4-H club lived on subdivision acreages that forbade them to keep pigs, so they kept their pigs at our house. A couple of pens behind our barn housed the pigs, and the kids came over on their bikes to replenish pig feed and check the automatic watering devices. One family of boys often brought their black dog along. On one such visit, they brought friends who also had dogs. I glanced out the window and screamed. Four dogs had packed Duncan, pinned him to the ground, and were at his throat.

"They're killing Duncan!"

Shane, sitting at the kitchen table, sprang up and was out the door. He streaked across the backyard toward the hog pens. It seemed impossible someone so bulky could be fleet. He had something in his hands; I couldn't see what. I was far behind, but running. Shane roared at the dogs and they dispersed. Shane ran after them and chased them from the yard.

I scolded the boys. "You can't bring your dogs here anymore! Leave the dogs at home."

"Okay."

Shane picked up Duncan and held him like a baby. Duncan was dripping with blood and saliva. We soothed and petted him, and Shane carried him to the house.

A small boy whom I didn't know looked at me with round eyes as he got on his bike.

"Did you see what that guy had in his hand?" he whispered.

"No."

"An ax!" His eyes got wider. "Was he going to use it on my dog?"

"I don't know."

"I would have sued." He pedaled off, glancing over his shoulder like he thought Shane might reappear.

Duncan had no deep wounds. We put antibiotic salve on the bleeding places.

Later I asked Shane, "Why an ax?"

"I didn't notice what it was. It was on the porch, I grabbed it."

"Would you have used it?"

"No. Well, maybe the handle, if the dogs hadn't run off. But, you know," he said soberly, "it was Duncan."

"Yeah." Any of us might have gone to an extreme to save Duncan.

Later, we saw the funny side. I told Mary and Matt, "Think of it from the boys' view. They look up and Goliath is thundering down on them with an ax in his hand."

"Their nine years of life flash before their eyes," Mary said.

The next day, Shane went to the 4-H'ers' home and told the boys he was sorry, he didn't mean to scare them. But the rest of the summer, the boys and their friends tied up their dogs before coming over.

THIRTY-ONE

....

Duncan chased the last of the lambs into the horse trailer and I slammed the door and latched it. I sat down on the fender, gasping. The fall morning had gotten warm. Duncan found a shady place beside the truck and flopped down, tongue hanging. From the trailer, bleating lambs made a commotion.

The night before, Mary and I had made an aisle of panels leading to the trailer. Once I got lambs penned in the barn, I only had to run them down the aisle to load them. That was if it went without a hitch, but complications nearly always arose when animals were involved. This morning it had been two balky lambs who had refused to load. While Duncan and I were coaxing them, other lambs decided they didn't like the trailer and returned to the barn. At one point I'd had all the lambs loaded but couldn't get a panel out of the way fast enough to close the trailer door, and all of the lambs had spilled out again.

Now we were loaded and ready to roll.

"Go get a drink, Dunc, then we'll leave." Duncan trotted off to a water tub.

I felt solemn as I drove to a meat plant in a nearby small town. The plant was offering above-market prices and the money would cover pressing bills, but delivering lambs to slaughter used to be George's job.

Earlier in the summer, we'd sold ewe lambs to a young breeder from the western side of the state. That had been gratifying because the man had studied our flock genetics. He was serious about making a living from raising sheep, and we felt pleased our good genetics would lay the foundation for his flock.

It had been a positive sheep year for us, but I dreaded delivering lambs to a meat plant. It wasn't as though I didn't understand the fate of wethers, the castrated males. I ate lamb, and it would have been hypocritical of me to disapprove of slaughtering animals. I tried for a chin-up attitude and climbed in the truck.

When I got to the plant, a man weighed my lambs, complimented me on their healthiness and leanness, and wrote me an invoice. My check would be mailed later that day. I went back to the truck, trying not to glance at the yard where the lambs had been penned. But as I began to pull out of the driveway, I looked in the rearview mirror. The lambs were lined up, innocent faces gazing through the wire fence. They stared at the trailer.

"Baaaa!" they called in loud voices.

I knew each of them and who their mother was. Some I'd helped bring into the world, and every one I'd met within minutes of its birth. One I'd nursed through a broken leg, changing the splint periodically until the leg healed.

I hit the brake. I couldn't ignore the scene in my rearview mirror. My lambs, shoulder to shoulder, bleating plaintively. I was their shepherd and they were asking me not to leave. Sheep know and love their homes, and these sheep knew they'd been uprooted and the person they depended on was leaving.

Except, wether lambs had a sure fate. I couldn't find a home for each of them as pets, though through the years I'd done that for wethers I'd gotten especially attached to.

I took my foot off the brake and began to ease forward. The truck veered out of the lane. I couldn't see the road because of tears.

I took a minute to blow my nose and wipe my eyes. Then I pulled back onto the driveway and hit the accelerator. I disciplined myself not to look back or in the rearview mirror. But it didn't help. The sight of the lambs staring after me, blatting pleadingly, had burned itself into my mind.

Out of sight of the plant, I pulled over and gave in to a good cry.

"I think I'm better now," I told Duncan after a minute. He looked woebegone himself.

I steered onto the highway. Tears kept coming.

The trip home took twenty-five minutes, and I didn't stop crying the whole way. Once, approaching a bridge, I almost clipped a guardrail.

Duncan leaned against me. Frequently, his tongue came out and slurped my wet cheek.

"I'll be okay when I get home," I told him.

But when I pulled into our driveway and saw our ewes grazing on the hillside, I felt miserable all over again.

The phone was ringing when I walked in.

"How did it go?" Will, who had become a dear friend, wanted to check how everything had gone. I couldn't answer. I simply cried.

At an earlier time, I'd been able to stop emotion, to trap it in a tight ball in my throat. I could smile when I felt crushed by grief. But I couldn't do the masks anymore.

"Can I help?" Will asked.

I finally managed to speak. "It's not right. It's not right to care for animals and know them as friends, then carry them off to a slaughter place." I slapped away tears. "They watch you pull away. They wonder where you've delivered them. We should stop raising farm animals. We should all be vegetarians."

He said, "You're upset and making big statements. Too big. We don't all need to be vegetarians and it's not wrong for people to raise animals for meat. But it may be wrong for *you*."

I stared at the phone as if I'd heard an oracle. What he said was entirely true. It *was* wrong for me.

Mary wasn't ready to get out of the sheep business yet, but I'd had a change of heart.

We began to thin the herd. We studied records and selected only the highest producers, and forced ourselves to get rid of some sentimental favorites. It had been a tearful thing to say good-bye to those ewes, but now every ewe on the place was an outstanding producer. We knew each one well.

The following spring, we had good weather for lambing, and once again, an abundance of multiples that included several sets of quads. We lost only two lambs to weather or mishap. The moderate weather continued, so when we carried out sheep tasks on the weekends, we didn't freeze and get miserable. One weekend, we gave shots and weighed lambs, another weekend we trimmed feet, the next weekend we did tails and testicles.

"We're really coming along," I told Mary. "Next weekend we'll take down the jugs and get the barn ready for summer. It's time to give another round of shots, and wean the lambs."

"Okay," she said.

But later that day she walked in the house, removed her muddy shoes, and announced, "Let's get rid of the sheep. All we do on weekends is work."

"Okay. Completely?"

"Let's keep only two," Mary said.

It was a difficult task to go through our records and decide which two young ewes carried the best genetics. But we did. One was from our Topaz line, one from our Emerald line. I put the rest for sale in the newspaper, and it took hardly any time before a buyer came for them.

The following year, we lambed out our two ewes and that was a breeze. They lambed in the morning, only a day apart, and had large, healthy quadruplets.

Though our maintenance on them and their lambs was low, we found we still couldn't get away for weekend camping and overnight events. Stray dogs in the neighborhood made us nervous. Also, we had to transport our ewes to a farm to be bred because it didn't make economic sense for us to keep a ram.

So when a Polypay breeder from Blackfoot came to buy sheep equipment and asked if we wanted to part with the last of our ewes, Mary and I gave it serious consideration. Dell had a sound breeding program, and he planned to keep our ewes separate. It was a way for our breeding program to go on.

And then, we were out of the sheep business.

I thought it would be a large adjustment because so much of our time, planning, and effort had gone into the sheep. I had an idea of myself as shepherd, and I enjoyed working outside with Mary. I had loved raising sheep and had warm memories of our sheep years, but to my surprise, I didn't miss them much. I marveled that we'd had time for them. I'd returned to school to finish a degree, I wrote a weekly newspaper column, and was working on a book. Mary danced three evenings a week. Mary would continue raising 4-H market sheep by purchasing lambs from sheep-raising friends.

Our talented and dedicated sheepdog no longer had sheep. But then, Duncan always had enjoyed his role as companion dog, too. It felt right to move on.

Winter

THIRTY-TWO

For February, the Sunday was unexpectedly sunny and beautiful. Ronna came out from town to join me for a country walk. Mary had gone to town with George to have lunch.

I took Gracie with us because she had few activities these days. Duncan still did morning and evening horse chores with me and sat beside me while I wrote at my computer. Gracie didn't like the house much and stayed in her pen except when I got her out for visits. Shane had reinforced her pen because she often tried to escape, now that she no longer had sheep to guard.

Gracie became ecstatic when she saw Ronna. She liked all small children, protected Mary and me from strangers, and was mildly aloof to everyone else. But she held three people outside the family in high esteem—Loy, a mother in our 4-H club; Will, who loved big dogs; and Ronna.

After our walk, Ronna and I sat on the porch enjoying the temperature, watching icicles melt. Gracie had her head on Ronna's knee. When it got chilly, we went into the house. Gracie eyed the sofa, bounded across the room, and jumped onto it. She stood atop it, wagging and smiling.

It was absurd, like seeing an elk or other huge animal standing on a living room couch.

"What's with you?" I asked, laughing. "You've never gotten on furniture before."

I pulled her off the couch, but her huge smile didn't falter; she seemed to think she'd made a good joke.

On Monday, a storm blew in and brought snow. Tuesday morning after I finished feeding the horses, I went to Gracie's pen. She was curled in a ball in a circular sheep feeder. On very cold nights or when it was windy, she slept in her doghouse, but on milder nights, Gracie chose the round feeder for sleeping.

"Gracie," I called. "Time to get up."

She didn't move.

I unlatched the gate and went to check her. She looked like a huge snowball, and her face had an expression of peaceful sleep. When I touched her, she didn't move.

I walked to the house like a robot. I sat down on the porch and stared at the frozen fields. Duncan sat beside me, eyes full of worry.

Gracie couldn't be dead. She had been healthy. The night hadn't been that cold. I wondered if her great, courageous heart had simply stopped. But she was only eight. I'd been concerned about Duncan, who was ten, because the books said Border collies burned themselves out at a fairly young age, but Gracie had shown no signs of hip problems, as many big dogs do, and she'd had no sign of illness.

I went upstairs to my computer and got on the Internet. I looked up "Great Pyrenees, life span." A Pyrenees Web site told me their average life was eight years. I scolded myself anyway. If I'd paid better attention, I might have saved her. If she'd had daily walks, instead of intermittent ones, she might have lived longer than average. I still had in my mind a picture from Sunday of Gracie standing atop the sofa, mouth open, canines gleaming. I'd never seen her act silly before, but I'd always been able to persuade her to "dance" with me in her pen, which consisted of her running wild, somewhat clumsy circles around me.

Though I knew it would be impossible, I went behind the barn and tried putting a shovel in the ground. The ground was ice. I had no idea what I'd do with Gracie's body.

I returned to Gracie's pen with Duncan. Duncan nosed Gracie's body, then sat down beside the feeder, solemn as a judge. I tried to lift Gracie's body, but it had frozen to the feeder. I turned the feeder on end and tried to ease Gracie free, but her limbs and hair were stuck. I wanted to avoid being rough with the body that had held her loving spirit, but Gracie's deadweight and the awkwardness of the feeder made it difficult to maneuver.

I went back to the house. A few hours of bright sunshine might warm things. Gracie would still be heavy, but then I'd be able to disengage her body from the feeder.

But the temperature hardly increased. The sky remained overcast and bleak, and on top of that, a wind had lifted.

Ronna listened politely on the phone while I recited lies. Except for Duncan, I'd never love another dog. I was going to move to town where life was simpler. Gracie's death was my fault.

When Mary returned from home, I still hadn't solved how to deal with Gracie's remains. The weather had grown more hostile. Now the wind was howling, and it had started to snow. The wind chill was brutal.

Blowing snow stung our faces when Mary and I went to Gracie's pen. Even with Mary holding the feeder and me pulling on the body, we couldn't dislodge her.

"Hot water?" I wondered.

We returned to the house, put on the teapot and more clothes, and after the water warmed, went back outside. I poured water gingerly at places where Gracie's body was stuck to the wood. Inch by inch, the limbs began to come loose. After a time, we had to go back in the house to heat more water and warm ourselves. The grimness of the situation took away any inclination to speak.

We kept on, easing each part of Gracie's body free. Finally, we were able to extricate it from the feeder.

"Now what?" Mary asked.

Good question. I'd heard of people who'd lost dogs during Idaho winter putting them in the freezer to await spring burial. That was out of the question for Gracie.

"The desert?"

Mary nodded.

Even with two of us, it took several minutes to drag the body to the truck and lift it into the bed. Ice, death, and Gracie's size made the body very heavy.

With snow blasting our windshield, we drove away from our neighborhood, past the farms located at the edge of the desert. We knew the nearby desert well because we rode our horses there. I remembered large lava outcrops, some with recesses or caves in them. Such a place could provide a sheltering spot for Gracie.

But the visibility was so poor we could see only the road ahead, lighted by our headlights, and nothing of the open fields. The farther we drove, the more difficult it became to see the road. We couldn't risk going farther.

"I wish we could find a rock enclosure," I said. I turned the truck so the headlights beamed on the fields. All we could see were bleak, white expanses with blowing snow.

The snow was getting deeper. We had four-wheel drive, but if we hit a drift, we could be in trouble. I pulled off the gravel road when we saw a windswept, open place that probably was the entrance to a dirt road. When we got out, wind and moisture slapped our bare faces. We let down the rear gate of the truck and pulled Gracie out. Again we tried for gentleness, but the difficulties of winter and her size made us harsher than we intended.

We laid her on a clean patch of snow. I tried to arrange her head so she would look the way I'd found her that morning, but all the tugging and lifting had taken the peaceful look from her face. She looked lonely and dead.

"Gracie, I'm so sorry about this," I said.

We could hardly get our breaths in the wind. We got back in the cab and sat in silence. For noble Gracie, who had kept watch over our sheep, it was a crass send-off.

"Should we go back and say some words over her?"

Mary pointed out the window at the white mound. "That isn't Gracie. Gracie's gone."

"Do we need to do something for us? For our grief?"

"Maybe tomorrow," Mary said.

We were numb and exhausted from cold and stress. We went home, drank hot chocolate, and stumbled off to bed.

The following day, Ronna arrived with pictures she had taken of Gracie. Gracie and me on the porch. Gracie snuggled up to Ronna's little girl, Stephanie. Gracie with my arms wrapped around her. Ronna had put the pictures in frames.

"If you'd like to," she said, "I'd enjoy hearing about Gracie's life. Where you got her, what she was like as a puppy, the times she ran off stray dogs."

Even with Ronna, it was hard not to be self-conscious about the tears and nose-blowing. But as I cried my way through Gracie stories, something rigid and painful in my belly started to dissolve.

When Mary and I were eating dinner, I suggested we do the same thing—share reminiscences about Gracie.

"Remember when we camped in that Montana valley people had warned us about? Told us not to go hiking because of the cougars?" I asked.

"But Gracie stuck to us like a tick, and we felt perfectly safe."

"We didn't just imagine we were safe, either," I pointed out. "We were safe."

"Safe in our tent, too, with Gracie lying at the entrance," Mary said.

Mary almost got tearful but fought for composure. I had cried so much during the past couple of days, I felt weak.

After a few minutes, we suspended reminiscing. Fourteen-year-old Mary seemed to roll with disappointment better than I. Maybe she had a more philosophical nature.

Yet, weren't some things in life, like losing a cherished dog, terribly sad? Did Mary mask things to her own detriment?

THIRTY-THREE

The scent of perfume engulfed the car.

"Geez," I said to Mary and her friend. "Did you use a whole bottle?"

Mary flashed a smile. "Oh Mom!"

Something began to gnaw at me. Usually, I would have waited until Mary and I were alone, but I jumped in.

"Are you smoking, Mary?"

"No-o-o!" Her expression changed to anger.

"Let me look at your eyes."

She glared at me.

"Smoking pot?" That would explain the wild amount of perfume.

"*NO!*"

I wanted, of course, to believe her. She'd always been honest to the point of being blunt.

I already kept track of her comings and goings, but I vowed to be more watchful. I already turned her down when she wanted to go to activities where parents wouldn't be supervising, but I didn't want to be a jailer, either.

A week later, a woman I knew from church phoned to tell me she'd seen Mary and a couple of girls at the drugstore during school hours. The girls had acted furtive; she thought they might be shoplifting. The woman took no pleasure in calling, she said; she had an interest in Mary.

When Mary got home I asked, "Were you in school today?"

"Of course."

"All day? Because I heard you were at the drugstore."

She blanched, then went on the offensive. "Shouldn't you trust your daughter more than someone who is trying to make trouble?"

I got a call from the school. Mary would be kept for after-school detention for taking five dollars from a girl's purse during gym class. When I picked up Mary from school she told me the girl had lied, but the gym teacher had said that Mary confessed. It was strange to think of Mary stealing. I left change around all the time, and it wasn't touched. A friend suggested an explanation; five dollars bought a hit of dope.

I'd worried about Mary when she went places on weekends and after school, but now I found it tough to keep my mind on studying and writing even when she was at school.

At ten one morning, the school's drug officer called. He had busted Mary for drinking. She'd been given a ticket and would have to go to court. Mary asserted it was the first time, she'd been unlucky and got caught. She didn't protest sterner restrictions I imposed.

One night as I was finishing chores, I noticed a car parked at the edge of our field, dimmer lights on. It could have been lovers or someone studying a map, but something told me it had to do with Mary. I went downstairs. She answered, "What?" when I knocked on her door. An icy breeze came from under the door. I opened it. The window in her downstairs room was wide open and a breeze was blowing in.

"What's going on?" I asked.

"I wanted a little air."

"It's winter."

"I was hot." Wearing a smirk, she closed the window. Later, through a 4-H friend, I learned she'd slipped out the window to make a drug buy. The hours when she was at home were no longer safe, either.

When her period of restriction was over, I allowed her to go to a party. She told me the location and we agreed to a curfew. The curfew came and went, and she didn't come home. I called her cell phone and she gave me a lame story about car trouble. I said I'd come get her. My longtime friend Dennis went with me. We couldn't find the address. I called her cell phone again. She gave me a different address.

When Dennis and I got to that street, a cop was parked at the end of it, parking lights on.

"This doesn't look good," Dennis said.

"What do you think is going on?"

"I'd guess the cops are watching a dealer."

I retrieved Mary from an upstairs apartment. She came along without resistance, but the following Monday she came home and scolded me because her friends believed I'd called the cops.

We didn't have ugly feuds. Mary handled her drug use a different way. In front of her friends, she'd hug me and say, "Mom! You're so *cute*. I *love* you." It was obviously fraudulent, even to a hopeful parent. Yet, I wanted to keep our relationship intact and hoped we could ride out this difficult time. I didn't realize the insidious nature of drugs, that people became obstacles to crawl over.

I jumped when the phone rang, day or night, fearing Mary had come to harm. The last years had brought difficult times—the divorce, my feeling of failure, and the wrenching experience of revisiting childhood abuse. But this was the worst.

I started attending Al-Anon meetings, and I listened to the counsel they offered. Take care of yourself, learn to let go, detach with love, take care of yourself. You can't save the loved one, take care of yourself. One gentle, loving woman recounted how she'd turned down her addict son's request to be admitted to her home on a cold night. She had forbidden him to enter her home when he was high, so she gave him blankets to sleep outside.

Close friends supported me once again. And there was Duncan. For me, life had become too grim to engage in play, but he didn't get that.

I was walking out to feed the horses. Duncan dropped onto his forepaws, wriggled his rear end in the air, and faced me with an expectant grin.

"No, Duncan," I muttered. I walked around him. He picked up a stick and ran to the hay stack, dropped the stick atop a bale, then backed up, expecting me to throw it.

"No, Duncan." I lifted an armload of hay and threw it over the fence to the horses. I started back to the house.

Duncan, stick in mouth, tore ahead of me. He dropped the stick onto the porch.

"Duncan, I can't—" It was hard to turn down someone so eager. "Okay, I'll throw it once."

Five minutes later, I was chasing after him, laughing.

I'd been investigating drug treatment programs and especially liked a wilderness program based in southern Utah. I'd planned to deliver Mary there after she completed a ballet performance she'd been rehearsing for, but she showed up at the dress rehearsal high. Her dance teacher told me, "Go ahead and take her. It will save me the trouble of kicking her out of the show."

Friends offered to take care of my animals. Mary drove off with me the next day, believing we were going to get her hair cut for the performance. When she realized we were on the highway going south, she screamed, "I can't miss the performance! This is the most important day of my life! You don't care anything about me!"

Duncan leaned over from the backseat, looking troubled, and tried to give her a consoling lick.

By the time we'd passed Salt Lake City, Mary had calmed down and even begun to chat a bit.

Mary, Duncan, and I stayed in a staff cottage that night, and the next morning, Mary and I affirmed we loved each other, and she knelt and said good-bye to Duncan.

The program operated on a belief that nature and natural consequences healed people. Mary lived in the wilderness for sixty days with minimal amenities and learned survival skills. But she turned out to be a tough nut to crack. At the end of the time, she hadn't acknowledged any problem. They sent her back to the wilderness. Another thirty days passed. One night at a campfire, a staff employee told about his parents' divorce and how it had affected him. For the first time, Mary gave in to tears. The staffer took Mary aside and the two of them had an emotional talk. It was a breakthrough. After another week, the staff added Mary's name to the list of those who would graduate.

Graduation weekend brought family members together with students to find new ways of dealing with each other. George drove to southern Utah; Matt and Shane flew in.

I camped in a tent at the edge of town. It was too warm to leave Duncan in the car and I couldn't leave him at the campground, so I asked permission from the conference's motel staff to tie Duncan in a shady area outside their building. Before a few hours had passed, motel maids had started bringing him leftovers and a hotel clerk was keeping his water dish full.

When Mary and the kids arrived from the field wearing cammies and reeking of campfire smoke, Mary spotted Duncan and yelled, "There he is!" Duncan wriggled with ecstasy. The kids who'd been with Mary had heard about Duncan and they made a fuss over him.

During sessions, family members who'd undergone tough months or years aired their complaints. Kids got a chance to tell their side of it.

During a break, I took Duncan for a walk in an open field behind the motel. "That's pretty heavy in there, Duncan."

Despite the hot day, Duncan sped off across the open field, creating an explosion of grasshoppers. He leaped a ditch and headed off for a stand of cottonwoods. When I caught up to him, I sat for a minute under the trees, breathing in the warm, dry air and the scent of mountain bluebells.

Sunday night, the counselors told me they didn't think Mary should return to her home community yet, and recommended she go to an extended-care facility in Louisiana. My heart sunk. I'd dreamed we would resume our former life. On top of that, Mary and I had a trip planned. Earlier in the year, Mary had successfully auditioned for a summer camp with the Colorado Ballet. I was going to drop her off in Denver and then go to a Western Writers of America confer-

ence in Colorado Springs. But the program counselors couldn't con-
done Mary being on her own in Denver. Sadly, I put her on a plane to
Louisiana.

*The conference hotel in Colorado Springs turned out to be a classy
resort.* I didn't know if they allowed dogs, so I checked in and settled
into my room, then sneaked Duncan up a back hallway. I ran into
novelists Kathleen and Michael Gear walking a pretty sheltie.

"They allow dogs, then?"

Michael said, "You paid your seventy-five-dollar dog deposit?"

"Um, no." I didn't have seventy-five dollars. Duncan would have
to keep a low profile.

But every time I took him out for a walk, someone noticed him.
Some members lived or had lived on ranches and had an admiration
for Border collies. Some came from eastern states and urban locations
and simply wanted to get acquainted with Duncan because he was so
outgoing and pleasant.

In the driveway one morning, a man in an elegant yellow sports
car threw on his brakes when he noticed Duncan. Duncan saw the
driver had an interest in him, ran to the car, and jumped up on it.

"No, Duncan." I pulled him off the car, not daring to examine
whether he'd left claw marks on the shiny yellow door. "I'm sorry,"
I said.

"Don't make him get down!" The man coaxed him up, ruffled
Duncan's hair, and told him he was handsome. The driver proceeded
to have a leisurely visit with Duncan, not noticing cars behind him
wanting to exit the driveway. Maybe out of respect for the make and
model of the car, no one honked.

"He's friendly! Is he just a puppy?"

"Actually, he's got some age on him."

"I hope I'll see you again, Duncan." To me he said, "Thank you so
much for letting him visit with me."

Like the motel staff in Utah, resort employees made friends with Duncan. When I got back to my room after attending panels, I'd find saucers on the floor.

"I hope you don't mind," a Hispanic girl said. "He's so sweet, I just have to share my lunch with him."

I tried to be inconspicuous taking Duncan out of the hotel for walks, but his new friends hollered across the lobby at him. At mealtimes, someone at my table would ask, "Aren't you the one with the black-and-white dog?"

"Yes."

"Well, I'm sending these two sausages to him."

At the Saturday night banquet, I sat at a table for twelve. A tall man in a cowboy hat announced, "This woman has the most polite dog you've ever seen." He said he was saving part of his steak, and the bone, for Duncan. A woman wanted to contribute something, too. The big man got a Styrofoam container from the waitstaff and sent it around the table. Steak bones, gravy, buttered rolls, bites of chicken breast all went into the container.

"There," the big man said. "Duncan gets a banquet, too."

I couldn't permit Duncan to eat all that rich food at once; he would have gotten sick. Though the enticing smells from the Styrofoam container kept Duncan's nose twitching, I parceled out the contents slowly during our drive back.

When we reached home I told Duncan, "If I'd been alone, I would have kept to myself, blue and dumpy. When you're along, I have no choice but to mingle."

THIRTY-FOUR

After a seven-year battle with cancer, my sister Bobbette entered hospice care in Florida.

She had vowed she would beat the disease, but the latest word from the doctors was, "There's nothing else we can do." Bobbette accepted the next phase with the grace she'd shown during her illness.

I went to Florida by train. When I arrived at Bobbette and Jack's home, a bald, skeletal-thin Bobbette looked up and said in a hopeful voice, "A miracle may still happen."

Jack and I got to be with her at the very end. It was a profound moment and a great gift for me.

Coming home from Florida, I got off the train in Louisiana and visited Mary. She was homesick for the West but working an AA program and committed to sobriety.

Jack and my nieces held two funerals—one in Florida, one in Colorado. When I got home, Duncan and I took to the road to go to Bobbette's Colorado funeral. Shane drove up from Texas in his small truck camper; Matt flew in from Berkeley, where he was in grad school.

With loss hanging over us like a shadow, Matt, Shane, and I all commented on Duncan's graying muzzle and the filmy cataracts forming over his eyes. One time when I came outside, Matt was sitting on a bench having a quiet talk with Duncan. Shane had a store of food in his camper that included a ham. He kept doling out ham to Duncan.

"Spoiling the dog," I observed.

Shane picked up Duncan and carried him against his shoulder. "There's no one like Dunkie."

A few months later, mortality did come stalking again, this time seeking Duncan.

Don, my writer friend, and I were giving a workshop at the Jackson Hole Writers Conference. After the conference, Tim, one of the organizers, hosted a cookout at his cabin.

I struck off on a hike with Duncan. The afternoon sun had warmed the mountains to a perfect temperature. As we climbed higher, the vegetation changed and I got an expanding view of the surrounding mountains. In one place where I stopped to catch my breath, the scene included an eagle riding a thermal next to a peak.

On a ridge, I sat atop a rock and caught my breath. Duncan sat as close to me as he could without crawling inside my skin. I breathed in the thin mountain air.

When I started down, Duncan sped ahead on the trail, though he came back regularly to check on me. I heard a creek roaring. Duncan looked back at me, lifted his ears, and got a happy, expectant face.

Snowmelt had swollen the creek. Duncan crouched on the bank and extended his muzzle. Sunlight shimmered on his black coat. He inched down to get a drink. In a flash, the creek reached up and pulled him in.

I ran to the bank, but the current had carried him off. I saw only his black-and-white head disappearing as the creek swept him away.

"Duncan!" I yelled, but the creek drowned my words.

I ran my fastest down the path, hoping to glimpse him. Trees and brush grew on the banks, but in open places I could see the creek. No Duncan.

I had no plan, just to try to keep up with the swiftly flowing water. My mind started trying to make tragedy bearable. If the creek claimed Duncan, maybe that would be how he wanted to go—on a perfect summer day in beautiful mountains. Maybe he would prefer that to decrepit old age.

Simultaneously I pleaded, "Don't die, Duncan."

I rounded a corner and saw a drenched Duncan trying to claw his way up the bank.

"Duncan!" I cried.

I got to him in an instant. He'd found the quietest place to try to escape the creek, but even there the water ran fast. Shrubs and weeds clogged the bank and blocked his escape. Only Duncan's front paws and head were free of the water, and he was scrambling, trying to get a toehold.

"Hang on," I yelled, and began uprooting plants. I flung them this way and that, clearing a space for him.

I lay on my stomach and reached for his collar. He stretched toward me. I got hold of him. I pulled. He fought like crazy to get footing on the slippery bank. With my free hand, I yanked out more weeds.

And then he was all the way out, gasping and soaked.

I lay on my belly, panting.

"Duncan," I said, and gave in to tears. "You scared me."

Drenched, he looked bony and smaller. He gazed at the ground without expression or even focus.

I got the leash from my jacket pocket and put it on his collar. "Let's get you to a warm spot," I said.

We left the tree-shaded path and climbed to a knoll so we'd be in sunshine. Duncan trotted beside me, listlessly, and didn't turn his head when I spoke. Maybe the icy creek had put him in shock; maybe he'd strained so hard to swim to safety, he was numb from exhaustion.

We walked on a sunny ridge back to the cabin. People were sitting in lawn chairs visiting. I scratched dried mud off my face, shirt, and pants. I found our host and told him what had happened to Duncan. Tim tied his own dog and went off to warn people who had children to stay far from the creek.

For an hour or two, Duncan lay in a patch of sunshine and slept. I felt concerned. When the sun changed position, Don carried Duncan to a new, sunnier spot.

Two boys started throwing a softball. Duncan opened his eyes and looked around. The vacant expression began to fade. He stood

up, ran to the end of his leash, and asked to be set free. I asked the
boys if they wanted a dog to join them and they did.

On the way home, Don said, "I might have lost you both today.
You wouldn't have gone in after Duncan, would you?"

"I don't think so." I'd grown up in Colorado and understood that
mountain creeks were powerful and deadly. The current had carried
Duncan away so quickly, jumping in to rescue him hadn't been an
option, but if it had happened more slowly, I couldn't be sure. It was,
after all, Duncan.

Duncan, sitting between us, looked over when Don spoke his
name. His sparkle had returned, and he looked vastly content. His
brush with death seemed completely behind him. I decided I would
put it behind me, too.

Yet, that night when I lay in my own bed with eyes closed, I reran
the awful footage of Duncan leaning over the creek bank, then being swept away, only his black-and-white head visible above the swift
water.

Mary came home. She resumed her activities but stayed away from the
friends she'd gotten in trouble with. I continued to attend Al-Anon.

I felt relieved and happy, but now I worried when I left to teach a
class at night or if I went out to dinner or a movie. When Gracie had
been alive, I'd had no concerns about leaving Mary alone. I'd felt
confident no intruder would ever get past Gracie. With his sensitivity, Duncan might have sensed and responded to danger, but all I'd
ever seen out of him was giddy hospitality. I started shopping for a
watchdog.

One morning when I went out to feed horses, I missed the ever-
present cat, Aurora. I called her and went searching. On the haystack
in the barn I found her lying dead, her face frozen in a snarl, ears
pinned to her head. I couldn't find injuries; it looked like something
had snapped her neck.

I came to the house and sat on the log bench. Rory, who had been a friend to all animals, even llamas. Rory, who liked to ride horses, tucked in front of me in the saddle. Rory, who'd trotted faithfully beside me as I did chores, even in miserable blizzards.

Aurora had always gotten along with dogs. I didn't know what or who had killed her, but a few mornings later, before it was fully light, I heard barking. I dashed to the barn and found Lala, the gray cat, hissing and moaning on a roof beam in the barn. The neighbor's rottweiler was on its hind legs, trying to climb a floor joist. I screamed at the dog and it ran off.

It seemed likely this was the dog who'd killed Aurora. Now I felt more convinced I needed to find a protective dog who would alert me to intruders. I got wind of a German shepherd/malamute in Pocatello up for adoption. I called and talked to the dog's owner.

"Does he get along with cats?" I would hang up if the answer was no. I had only Lala left, but my neighbors had cats and I didn't want a dog who would pose a threat to them.

"Gets along with all animals," the man said. He was a bachelor, being transferred for work, and couldn't take the dog. He'd had the dog, Chakra, since it was a pup, and it was now seven months old. The dog loved to play in the park and go for rides. "He's the best dog I've ever had," the man said.

"Is he protective?" I asked.

"No," he answered. "But he's large and has one blue eye, and he looks intimidating. A lot of people think he's part wolf."

The dog already was in foster care with four other dogs and several cats. I was scheduled to take a three-hour exam at Idaho State University on the works of William Shakespeare. Because I'd be in Pocatello for the test, I figured it wouldn't hurt to stop and meet the dog.

After a twenty-two-page-long test, I was exhausted by the time I drove to the dog's foster home.

The big dog nearly knocked me over with his friendliness. He had German shepherd black-and-tan coloring, but a thick rug of a coat and the size of a malamute. House cats came and went and the dog merely smiled at them. All adoptions were on a trial basis, so I decided to take him home and see how he fit in.

Famished, I stopped for a hamburger at a fast food place. I worried the dog, having had so much recent change, would be upset at being alone in a strange place. I bolted down the burger and rushed back to the car. The dog, spread over the entire backseat, was asleep.

His foster family had been calling him Doofus; before that he was Chakra. I didn't like either. When I got in the car, the dog woke up. I asked him which name he liked. "Chakra?" "Doofus?" He didn't respond.

I tested a list of names, seeing which he might react to. Rudy? Loren? Hollingsworth? My test still played in my head. Shakespeare?

The dog lifted his paw and placed it on my arm.

When we got home, I sat on the porch facing him and tried again. Buddy? Randolph? Nelson? Shakespeare? He lifted his giant paw and rested it in my hand.

"I guess you want to be Shakespeare," I said.

I introduced Shakespeare to Duncan, who growled at him. Shakespeare lay on his back and submitted. Duncan didn't like dog competition, but this big galoot would respect his seniority. Lala, the gray cat, also established herself over the giant.

Not often does an animal make it so clear what he wants to be called. Whenever I spoke his name, Shakespeare responded by putting his paw on me. Days later, after Mary and I had become accustomed to the name, I realized something. The dog had been taught to "shake" and thought I was asking him to do a trick.

One evening as I sat at my computer, Shakespeare kept putting his head on my keyboard. He made it impossible for me to work and I was getting annoyed. Finally, his oversize claws scraped the skin on my forearm.

"Ouch!" I said, and flicked out my hand. My fingertips grazed Shakespeare's muzzle.

Shakespeare let out a whine and scrunched his eyes shut. He retracted his neck into his shoulders and fell over on his side. He stretched out on my office floor, covering his eyes with his great paw.

Matt, who was home for the summer, said, "Hamlet!"

"I barely touched him," I said.

Matt asked, "What would you expect from a dog named Shakespeare?"

THIRTY-FIVE

....

"We've come to the end of the world, Duncan."

Duncan looked out the truck window. Sagebrush stretched as far as the eye could see in every direction, interrupted only by lava outcrops. Fifty yards off, three elk sauntered past.

"Pretty soon, we'll fall off the edge," I predicted.

Duncan wagged happily.

The path we sat on was little more than tire tracks. However, we weren't lost. The census map in my lap showed exactly where we were. Except the census map believed I was on an actual road. And the Census Bureau believed a tiny square at the end of this road might be a house where people lived. My boss, Jack, had warned that the aerial photos the Census Bureau used for mapping may have been interpreted by people who couldn't envision western distances and isolation. The square I was trying to find might be an abandoned trappers' cabin or even a portable cow or sheep camp. No one had been on this road in years.

I was working in a county as large as some foreign countries, populated by 800 people. We, as census workers, were determined to find every one of them. I liked the democratic idea that every single person counted. And I could hardly believe my good fortune— getting paid to explore isolated country. I wore jeans and T-shirts to work and got to spend the whole day with my dog. At night, I squeezed in some productive writing hours because I felt refreshed from being outdoors.

The previous day I'd driven my car and worried every minute it might break in two on the rutted paths. Today, I'd come with Flora, my thirty-year-old truck. I still had to be careful and drove only 5 mph, and even at that speed, Duncan pitched and rolled on the seat next to me, finding it impossible to stay upright.

I stopped and took out a cheese sandwich, half for me, half for Duncan. I ate both cookies and the apple and poured water for both of us. We had twenty minutes left on our break.

"Come on, Duncan."

I climbed down from Flora, and Duncan and I started across the empty range. Duncan ran to the top of a rock outcrop, looked back, and wagged an invitation. I searched for a path in the thick sage-brush. Rattlers might be sunning themselves, so I picked my way.

I used binoculars to search for the tiny square the map showed. The view from the outcrop was not encouraging. No sign of human life anywhere, but we spotted a jackrabbit, found an owl pellet, and listened to birds twittering in the brush. A drab brown female sage grouse crossed our path.

Thirty minutes later, the road ended. A lava ridge blocked me from going forward and rocks and sagebrush hemmed me in on either side. I got out and climbed another lava outcrop. I saw in the glasses a trapper's cabin that hadn't been occupied for a hundred years.

I turned Flora around and headed back the way we had come. I was tired now, and the road seemed harder to negotiate. I spotted a cowboy seated on a horse in the far distance. If I had a breakdown, I could walk for help.

It was nearly dark when I got back to the main road. Duncan gave up on scenery, laid his head on my thigh, and slept.

I met dogs of every size, shape, color, and breed, and that added to the pleasure of census work. In rural areas, I sometimes worried when dogs streamed to the driveway, barking and growling. Duncan barked and growled back. My coworkers had horror stories about dogs. In one case, a family had stood by while their dog took a hunk from an enumerator's thigh. The woman had had to slam her census note-book on the dog to make it let go.

But I'd been lucky. When I opened my car door and addressed the dogs: "Hi, cutie. Is anyone home?" or, "Go on, you noisy thing," I'd so far encountered only friendliness. I'd long believed that country dogs had healthier minds than dogs cooped up in town, yet, when I began to enumerate on residential streets, I continued to meet agreeable dogs.

After completing a block, I would return to the car and catch up on paperwork. Duncan would nose my hands and clothes. "What is this fresh dog scent?"

"A nice dog," I'd say. "But didn't hold a candle to you."

Though Idahoans could be characterized as distrustful of the federal government, a large number knew the U.S. Constitution required a decennial census. Most people treated enumerators hospitably, even if they found our questions nosy. But not every encounter turned out to be pleasant.

One day I was working alone in a rough neighborhood. In our mostly middle-class town, I'd never seen streets like these. Broken whiskey bottles, trash, and toys hid the sidewalks. It was hard to find my way across the yards. The sun had gone down, and daylight was fading. I had only two more houses to visit, so I decided to finish before going home.

The small house had no panes in the windows. A ragged dish towel hung as a curtain in one window frame. I opened a broken yard gate and had trouble replacing the latch. Then I saw the dog. It was short, perhaps a pit bull, and airborne, flying toward me.

It was a completely silent attack. The dog had leaped off the ground and was coming at my face or throat. Remembering how my coworker had defended herself, I lifted my hardcover notebook as a shield. The dog hit it with a smack. The dog fell back, stunned, but struggled to its feet.

At that moment, a young woman screamed at the dog. The dog slunk over to her. She grabbed it by its collar, swore at it, and flung it into the house.

She said. "Who you looking for?"

I shook my head; I couldn't speak. Woodenly, I walked out the gate and latched it. My legs felt like soggy noodles. I reached my car, got in, and locked it, frightened of everything on that street. I drove several blocks to a well-lighted parking lot, shut off the car, and hugged Duncan.

When I was promoted to supervisor it clipped my wings, but my pay increased. By then, Duncan had become accustomed to going to work with me every day. When I tried to leave in the mornings, he would stand by the car, ears up, face endearingly expectant. Many days I couldn't turn him down and took him along to the office. I left him in the car, but on my lunch break, I walked him and gave him water.

Mark, who tended the front desk, noticed Duncan peering out the car window. "Do you leave your dog out there all day?" he asked.

"He begs to come along, and he's fairly content in the car."

"He's a pretty dog." It was Mark's job to make sure that anyone coming in the front door had a census badge. The Census Bureau had promised the public confidentiality and no one was permitted to go past Mark's desk.

Mark searched in his drawer and brought out a temporary badge and a marking pen. "What's your dog's name?"

"Duncan."

Mark wrote on the badge, then went to my car. He let Duncan out, attached a Census Bureau badge to his collar, and invited him to come in.

"We have a mascot now. Duncan, the Census Dog."

"Everybody counts," I said.

Duncan ran to my desk. I told him "down" and "stay." He did, gazing around with perked ears.

Clerks came by to pet him. Mark and I hadn't exactly sneaked him in, but the dog lovers in the office seemed to understand it would be a good idea to keep his presence quiet.

My supervisor walked past my desk, stopped, and backed up.

"Yours?" she asked.

I nodded. I was going to offer to take him back to the car, but she said, "What beautiful manners he has." She knelt and petted him, then walked on.

It would have been pushing things to make Duncan a permanent fixture, but many days, Mark would slap a badge on Duncan's collar, and Duncan would trot into the office. Ken, in charge of supplies, made sure Duncan had fresh water. Other clerks would come to my desk and silently hold up cookies. I would shake my head. They showed up with meat scraps. I'd nod. With his unfailing sense of what was appropriate, Duncan lay beside my desk or sat beside my chair perfectly still. If he got up to explore, I could whisper to him to return and he did.

Once or twice, the big boss came and stood beside my desk and discussed some work matter. I don't know if he didn't notice Duncan, or if he'd signed on to the Duncan-in-the-office conspiracy.

Outside the office, Duncan the Census Dog continued to ride with me when I went to small towns to administer tests for employment and distribute publicity. It was a peaceful, pleasant time. I missed Mary, who had gone to southern Utah to work as a wilderness instructor, and Matt and Shane, who were in college. But Duncan and I had blue-sky days of driving around on country roads, spotting great blue herons, eagles and deer, and watching horses play in pastures.

One morning I turned on the faucet and no water came out. I called my well repairman. Later that day, he called me at work.

I needed not one new well pump, but two. A ground source heat pump heated my house and that pump was shot, and so was the one that supplied water to the house. I asked what two pumps would cost. When I hung up, I sat in silence.

Harvey, who sat across from me, said, "That didn't sound good."

I told him about the pumps.

"How will you pay for them!"

"I don't know." I added, "I'm not worried." For some inexplicable reason, the pump calamity hadn't sent me into a panic. Maybe the preceding years had taught me that things work out.

Only a day later, I received a message to come for an interview with a company that supplied technical editors to government contractors. The company was hiring editors to go to Las Vegas. Linda, the company's co-owner, told me the Las Vegas job paid well and editors were housed at company expense in an apartment complex with three pools and a workout facility.

"I can't leave my elderly dog," I said. I had three dogs, actually—Duncan, Shakespeare, and Mimi, Mary's white Border collie.

"The apartments allow pets," Linda said. "Several of our employees have them. If your dog doesn't like apartment living, he can go to day care, which is located close by."

But I had the horses to consider, too, along with the other two dogs. Besides, I didn't want to live in a city with noise and crowds.

"We'd need you to be down there in a week," Linda said.

That night I told my friend Debbie about the job offer. "I do have two well pumps to pay off."

"Maybe it could work," she said. Her daughter, Joey, was getting married, and she and her new husband might like to have a country place for a while.

That sounded too good to be true. Farm-raised kids to watch the house. When Debbie checked with them, they said they'd be happy to care for Shakespeare and Mimi, the cat, Lala, and the horses, Rainbow and Meg.

Mary came in from the wilderness on a break and called home. I told her about the offer.

"How fun!" she said. "I'd rather come to Las Vegas to visit than to Idaho Falls."

Rick, a census clerk, said to me on Monday, "I hear you're moving to Las Vegas."

"Yes."

"What will you do there?" He frowned over his thick glasses.

"I'm going to fulfill a lifetime ambition and become an exotic dancer."

Without blinking, Rick replied, "I always knew this little town was too small to hold you."

When my census friends gave me a going-away party, they served a cake molded like a female torso, gave me a platinum wig, and a purple feathered boa. Above the refreshment table hung a pair of coveralls with balloons and ribbons attached in suggestive places. I posed for pictures wearing the wig, the boa, and the coveralls.

A week later, my small car, loaded with computer and printer, a few paintings, pictures of the kids, and Duncan in the passenger seat, pulled out of my driveway and headed south. Duncan, retired sheepdog; Duncan, recipient of letters from children; Duncan, census mascot; would soon become Duncan, Urban Collie.

THIRTY-SIX

I rested my head against the swimming pool's cement wall. It was an April night, but the temperature was in the nineties. Around me, strangers from my apartment complex visited with each other.

"You know what I love about Las Vegas?" A woman with a breathless voice directed her question to me.

"What?" I asked.

"The night sky." She pointed. Down on the Strip, searchlights beamed cylinders of light into the sky in the colors of hot pink, dayglow green, and purple.

I smirked. "Right."

I looked again at the woman. She was serious.

The gaudy sky, so different from the twinkling canopy of stars in Idaho, wasn't the only thing I'd found to dislike. I didn't like the weather, the noise, the traffic. And I wasn't the only one.

On our first day in Las Vegas, Duncan refused to drink anything. Duncan, a farm dog who had drunk from rank puddles, rusted containers, and brackish ponds, gave me a reproachful look when I set a dish of Las Vegas water before him. But when I bought him bottled water from the store, he drank it. I didn't think the tap water tasted bad, but if Duncan turned it down, I wasn't going to drink it, either.

On the first day of my new job, I showered and had breakfast, then took Duncan for a walk at 7 A.M. Even in light clothing, I came home sweating and had to change clothes.

The next day, I took Duncan for a walk at six, then ate breakfast, showered, and dressed. That worked better. At that hour, the temperature was beautiful, and I wore a T-shirt and shorts. But if I needed to walk Duncan at 6 A.M. in April, what time would I be getting up in July?

I checked with the downstairs neighbor who was home during the day to find out if Duncan had barked or created any nuisance. She said she hadn't been aware there was a dog upstairs. Duncan, it appeared, would be content at the apartment, where he could have the whole place, and not have to go to day care where he would be kenneled.

Still, I saw something would have to change in Duncan's habits. At home, I'd been letting Duncan out at three or four in the morning to pee. His senior bladder didn't allow him to hold on all night. In the wee hours he would lay his nose on my pillow and nudge my face. I would follow him downstairs, let him go outside, and wait while he relieved himself. Then the two of us would trudge back upstairs, and I would fall back into bed. It interrupted my sleep very little.

Now I lived in an upstairs apartment next to a four-lane highway. A younger Duncan could have gone out to pee alone, because he had responded well to voice commands. But Duncan's sight and hearing had failed so much, even on the farm I'd kept my eye on him so he didn't wander into danger he couldn't see or hear.

Long years before, when he was a pup and I needed his help in keeping the sheep back when I fed, I'd sat down and talked to him and explained my problem. I tried that again.

"Duncan," I said. "It isn't safe for me to take you out in the night. I don't know how you're going to do it, but you're just going to have to hold it."

His filmy eyes looked into mine. Incredibly, he didn't ask to go out at night anymore. Good thing. On our morning walks, I came upon shattered liquor bottles, mountains of beer cans, and puddles of vomit. A lot of partying was going on in the complex while I slept.

Only once did Duncan ask to be let out in the night. I awoke to find Duncan's nose an inch from mine. He fidgeted and moved toward the bedroom door. I looked at the clock. It was 3 A.M.

"Can't, Toto. We're not in Idaho Falls anymore."

He came back and put his face on my pillow, wriggling with despair.

I sighed. What was I supposed to do?

I pulled on shorts and a top and took him outside. It felt very dark. Duncan ran to an area thick with bushes and lifted his leg

Without turning around, I became aware someone was behind me. I moved to the end of Duncan's leash to get myself into a more open spot, then turned around.

A kid about thirteen, in shorts big enough to accommodate two more kids, stood beside the building, hands in his pockets.

"Can I pet your dog?"

"Sure."

"Is he friendly?"

"Yes."

The kid came over and dropped to his knees. He ruffled Duncan's head, and Duncan lay down and exposed his belly. The kid gave Duncan a tummy rub. It looked like any heartwarming boy-and-dog scene, except that it was 3 A.M. in a city. I wondered if this kid's mother knew he was out.

"Thanks," he called after me. "Nice to meet you, Duncan. Good-bye."

Duncan met other kids. A pie-faced African-American boy about five years old started showing up beneath my balcony in the evening, calling, "Can Duncan come out and play?" I would take Duncan downstairs to the grassy area where the boy and his friends waited.

The boys saw no need for me to come along, but with Duncan's infirmities and the constant traffic moving through the complex, I didn't feel I could leave him in the care of young children. Even so, after a few minutes, the boys would forget I was there and be deeply absorbed in their tail-wagging neighbor.

Though he was an old dog, Duncan was used to running around the farm and still had lots of energy. I, who sat at a computer all day, needed exercise, too. Near the apartments, a man-made lake lay next to upscale homes in a gated community. A three-mile path around the lake offered a quiet, green place to take Duncan walking.

Though lonely for my friends, the farm, outdoor Idaho, and my other animals, Duncan and I became a part of a dog-walking world inhabited by warm, friendly people. I wondered if dogs supplied a way for people to interact in a city populated by many newcomers. In Idaho Falls, custom had dictated that people keep their dogs apart on the riverside path. But on the lake walk, people politely asked, "Is it all right if my dog meets your dog?" Duncan, who always had gotten along well with other animals, loved the new practice.

A pair of greyhounds strolled the path every morning, walking with two people who carried industrial-sized coffee mugs. The greyhounds and Duncan hit it off at once, and whenever Duncan saw them appearing over a green rise, he would tug on his leash and wag. I learned that the people, plump and mellow, took the greyhounds, fit and hollow, to a nursing home three times a week.

A young man who lived in a nearby building had two German shepherds. One, a female, skulked and acted leery; the other, a male, was gregarious and outgoing. Duncan became friends with both dogs.

"I've never seen her like another dog," the man said when the female ran to the end of her leash and accepted Duncan's invitation to play.

There was one exception to the cordial dog atmosphere. Every morning we encountered a burly, mean-looking Akita. The dog would begin a deep growl when he spotted us, drop his ears, and narrow his eyes. Duncan, normally confident, would move close to me.

The Akita walked at the side of a frail old woman who was barely taller than the dog.

"I've . . . got . . . him," she would call in a quavery voice. I didn't feel assured.

We lived far from the life Duncan had grown up with, yet he showed the same happiness in the mornings I'd always seen. In heat like he'd never felt before, with traffic noise all around, he still tried to get me to play. He would run to the end of his leash, turn and look, dash back to me, and be off again. I understood I was supposed to chase him. I could last only a half block or so before I got too hot, but Duncan seemed content with that abbreviated version of his game.

Sandy, who lived in the building next to me, said, "I like to watch you and Duncan go by in the morning. I don't think I've ever seen a dog prance like he does. Is he just a puppy?"

One night when Duncan and I were walking between apartment units, a young man peered over a balcony. Then he hurtled down the outside stairs.

"This is the dog I want!" He called up to his friends, whom he had abandoned on his porch, "Come down and see this dog. This is a *Border collie*." Soon Duncan was surrounded by people. Despite his poor vision, he still peered into the eyes of each person.

The guy asked, "Is it true they're so smart?"

"Yes."

"Is this the kind you see on TV herding sheep?"

"This dog used to herd sheep."

"*This* dog did?"

"He's retired now."

"This dog *actually* herded sheep? Like, in trials?"

"No. We raised sheep. He was indispensable to us."

"That was his job? Mike! Stephanie!" He hollered at the few people who'd remained on the balcony. "Get down here! You gotta see this dog."

I was used to Duncan attracting people because of his personality and intelligence, but in Idaho, Border collies were a common sight riding in the beds of pickups. It surprised me that some people had never seen a Border collie up close.

The partygoers swarmed Duncan for fifteen minutes, asking how livestock people trained their dogs, whether Border collies could live successfully in town, if Duncan knew any tricks. What a show we could have put on a few years earlier, before his vision had failed and his hips began to hurt. He could have wowed them with tricks like jumping through a hoop and walking on his hind legs. He could have spiraled six feet into the air to catch a Frisbee. I could have demonstrated the number of words he understood.

Even so, meeting a real sheepdog, and one as personable as Duncan, pleased these people no end. They went back to their party with reluctance.

Mary came out of the Utah wilderness eager for a visit to the glittering city of Las Vegas. She arrived late one evening and only then realized she'd left my address and phone number behind. She remembered some of the instructions from our phone conversation. It took her awhile to extricate herself from the snarl around the Strip. Then she found a road, took a stab, and, incredibly, the road brought her to my apartment complex.

By now it was 2 A.M. She saw that the complex had twenty or so buildings, but, once again, with great luck, drove right to an open area she recognized from my description during our phone conversation. She stood on the grass facing one building, her back to another. Each building had eight units in it. She wondered how she could find my apartment without knowing the number.

An idea hit. From her place on the lawn she called in a hopeful voice, "Duncan? Duncan!" She had forgotten about Duncan being deaf. Blue, my next-door neighbor Karen's dog, heard the call and started barking. Mary ran up the stairs to our landing. She paused, wondering which unit the barking came from. I'd been sleeping lightly and opened the door and greeted her. Duncan, who'd slept through it all, woke up, happy to find Mary standing in our living room.

The next morning, Karen called to me from the grassy area where residents took their dogs. "I hope Blue didn't waken you in the night. I don't know what got into her."

Mary and I made plans to rendezvous for camping and hiking in southern Utah. Southern Utah, home to beautiful rock spires and formations, became a furnace in summer, but in spring it offered perfect temperatures. When we'd had sheep, our springs had always been too busy to go there.

We arrived at our agreed-on location on a Friday night. Saturday morning we awoke to magnificent scenery and perfect weather, but something happened when we were hiking that sobered me.

Mary and I were trudging on an open, sandy stretch. Duncan, who had been apartment-bound for a month now, was a black-and-white streak, zooming from left to right across our path. Periodically, he would ease down to the shallow river and get a drink.

Mary and I stopped to rest on a wide rock ledge. The ledge lay two to three feet lower than surrounding land. Duncan came on the run to join us. He didn't slow when he reached the end of the dirt and a moment later went *kersplat* onto the hard ledge. He lay blinking and stunned.

"Duncan, didn't you see the edge?" Mary asked. He hadn't. I hadn't been able to figure out how blind Duncan was because he sometimes barked or wagged at people who were a huge distance away. It was evident he had little vision left. The rest of the weekend, whenever we neared terrain with overhangs or steep places that might offer hazards to a blind dog, I clipped a leash on him.

"I hate to do this," I told him. Even in this place where cars presented no threat, he couldn't be free in the old way.

I made a promise to him.

"Duncan, when it stops being fun, I'll call a halt to it. You won't have to suffer."

Shelley, another editor from Idaho Falls, sometimes went on evening walks with Duncan and me. Shelley had gone to a pet store and laid in a supply of dog treats. Duncan's love of food hadn't failed a bit, and when we got to Shelley's building, he would surge up the stairway, dragging me with him.

When Tammy, another new editor, moved into Shelley's apartment building, we had a third person to join us for walks. With this bigger group, Duncan now had a Border collie dilemma. He needed to keep the walkers together. If Duncan and I walked ahead, he dragged, looking back and yearning to gather up the stragglers. If I walked behind, he strained to move ahead so the leaders couldn't get away. Tammy and Shelley indulged him on this and tried to stay close to me. Then Duncan would relax and walk contentedly, satisfied that his flock of walkers was bunched.

Mornings got progressively hotter and I moved our exercise time to 5:30 A.M. A few weeks later, I had to move our walk to five. I dressed in a sports bra and shorts and wondered what I'd wear when it got hotter. How much skimpier could I get?

I made friends with Kirk, a recent transplant from the Northwest, who liked to hike and welcomed Duncan along. Red Rocks Park was eight miles from my house. On a weekend, if we left early, Kirk and I could have a hike behind us before going out to an abundant casino breakfast. Remembering the episode in Utah when I was hiking with Mary, I kept Duncan on a leash near precipitous edges. But much of the time Duncan could run free, and during those times, would nearly turn inside out with ecstasy. It did me good to see him enjoying himself so much.

But in this desert place, Duncan had to contend with hot sand. He stopped frequently on the trail to gnaw his paws, trying to get rid of fine sand that crept between his toes. At a pet store, I found expensive doggy hiking booties, but I doubted Duncan would be willing to leave them on. Instead, I bought him children's socks and secured them in place with ponytail holders. I usually had to put them back on three or four times during a hike because they fell off or he pulled them off. Still, they helped.

I'd scarcely been separated from Duncan in the fourteen years I'd had him. He'd gone along on research trips, to writing conferences, to my sister's funeral. In Vegas, I waited to do errands until the sun went down so Duncan could ride along in the car.

But he would not get to go to Shane's graduation from college. I needed to fly to Texas because I could take only a couple of days off work.

People left pets in the care of kennels all the time, but I worried Duncan might be bereft. He'd adapted to apartment life with his usual aplomb, but that may have been because he made himself at home wherever I was. If I left town and he was confined in a kennel, only being let out periodically into intense heat, would he decide he'd lost everything? How would he know I'd be coming back?

I finally called a nearby vet clinic that boarded dogs and scheduled a checkup for Duncan. But *I* planned to do the real checkup—on the place and the vet.

The vet, a hearty guy named Bill, had spent time in Idaho. He lifted Duncan onto the examining table.

"How old is this dog?"

"Fourteen."

"No!" He ran his hands over Duncan's body. Duncan smiled at him.

"I hope I have a bod like this when I'm that age."

"It's not an ordinary dog," I said.

"No, he's a fine guy."

"He's famous, actually."

"Mmm."

"Duncan used to get letters from kids all over the U.S."

"Hmm."

Did he think this dog with a gray muzzle and little hearing and eyesight was any old dog?

"He used to be a working sheepdog."

That caught the vet's interest. "Really?" He said to Duncan, "Where did you ranch, buddy?"

We eased into a comfortable conversation about sheepdogs. When we had exhausted that topic, I made the situation uneasy again.

"How do you discipline dogs here?"

The vet gave me a blank look. "We have no occasion to discipline dogs."

"I mean your staff, do any of them . . . um, hit dogs?"

"We have an excellent, dog-loving staff. Harvey, the manager of the kennel, is magic with dogs."

"I've never left this dog at a kennel before. I'm worried he might not know I'm coming back. Do dogs ever die of broken hearts?"

"I've been in practice a long time, and I've never seen it. There's a lot of activity going on here. Other dogs walking past, the staff checking on them. He'll be a little sad for a few hours, then he'll think it's an interesting place."

I knew I sounded fidgety; despite that, I went on.

"There's a fatty deposit on his belly. It's been the same size for years, hasn't grown. You wouldn't try to operate on it, would you?"

"I wouldn't operate on a dog this age in any case."

"Can I leave a Texas phone number, and would you call me if he seems despondent?"

He said he would.

I did a test run. Kirk and I wanted to climb Mount Charleston on the outskirts of town. It would be an all-day hike, very arduous, and we needed to carry all our water. Several places were very steep and Duncan would have had to be on a leash most of the day.

So on a Friday night I deposited Duncan at the vet's. I met Harvey, the kennel manager, who was a jolly guy.

"C'mon in, Duncan. We got a place for you."

I started into my spiel. "He's never been left at a kennel. He doesn't see much, he's deaf. He's not really used to the area or the heat, either."

Harvey ran a dog biscuit under Duncan's nose. Duncan started to follow him.

"Nothing wrong with his nose!" Harvey said.

I picked Duncan up on Saturday night, and the receptionist said he'd done fine. He'd liked the walks around the block and showed great interest in the other dogs.

A week later, I left for Shane's graduation, still a little concerned about Duncan. But after arriving in Texas, I got involved in graduation activities.

Still, when I returned, I could hardly wait to pick up Duncan.

When he ran out from the back and jumped up on my leg to greet me, I felt great relief.

One morning on my lake walk, I had an experience that filled me with longing. Duncan and I were walking around the lake when a black-and-white Border collie streaked past.

I was astonished. What was a Border collie doing out alone?

Duncan saw the dog and whimpered.

The dog darted to the intersection, then plunked down, and sat. A minute later, a car drove up with its windows down. A person called out the window, "Okay." The dog dashed across the intersection, then streaked over the green hillside until he reached the next intersection, sat down, and waited for the car to catch up.

Apparently, the dog had too much energy to be walked the conventional way, so the person had taught the dog to stop at intersections, wait until it received permission, and then continue.

I looked at Duncan, who at that moment was panting from the heat, and thought of his former life chasing sprinklers and sheep, biting snowdrifts on frosty mornings, hiding behind a haystack and jumping out to frighten me.

I stopped and knelt beside him. "I promise, I'll get you home."

THIRTY-SEVEN

At a Monday morning staff meeting, the boss announced that because of cutbacks, all temporary help would be let go. Other editors left the meeting with worried frowns. I hid a grin. I'd almost paid for my well pumps.

The next morning, the boss showed up at my desk. She gestured for me to follow her to her office. She said in a low voice. "Don't worry. We're going to keep *you*."

I tried to smile.

Two weeks later, another memo went around, saying all subcontractors would be let go. I called the company I worked for and was told to ignore the memo until someone handed me a pink slip. But it looked like I'd soon have a book contract with a regional publisher. I calculated finances one night and speculated how long the money I'd saved might last. The next day I called Joey, my tenant, asking if it really would be okay if I came home, though I'd said I'd be gone until December. She said she understood my need to get back to Idaho. I went in the next day and gave two weeks' notice.

I sat on the balcony that night brushing Duncan, feeling like it would be hard to stay inside my skin while two weeks passed.

After my long drive home, Duncan and I had a jubilant reunion with the Idaho animals. Shakespeare and Mimi sniffed Duncan, then tore in circles in the dog yard. Lala, the cat, stroked herself against Duncan's chest. Lala had been ailing, but Joey had wormed her, and she looked better than when I'd visited in July. "Thanks for staying alive,"

I told her. "I told you I'd get back." Duncan and Rainbow touched noses while I saddled the mare, then Duncan trotted along when Rainbow and I went for a ride.

The regional publisher went out of business, and my potential contract disappeared, but an Idaho Falls temp agency called and asked if I'd be interested in a five-month technical editing job. I could work a few months, then take some months off to write.

Duncan and I ambled down the road, heading home from a walk. I was admiring yellow and orange fall colors on Taylor Mountain and savoring the crisp temperature of an Indian summer day. Duncan trotted at a good pace. He'd shown a surge in vitality since we'd returned to Idaho. Escaping the Las Vegas heat and being back in the country had done wonders for his energy.

A faded dump truck, loaded to overflowing with freshly dug potatoes, pulled up beside us. The truck's engine labored noisily and leaking fluid sent out an awful smell.

The man in the cab, square-faced with a thick neck, called down, "Excuse me."

I moved over to the rumbling truck. The driver probably needed directions, and I, recently returned resident of the road and brimming with goodwill, would be happy to supply them.

"Border collie?" he asked over the engine noise.

"Yes."

"What's his name?"

"Duncan."

"Hi, Duncan."

"I'm afraid he's pretty deaf."

"Beautiful dog."

"He's a really good dog."

The man reached his beefy arm out the truck window, extending a closed fist.

"Can he have this?" He opened his hand, and in it lay a dog biscuit.

"Sure." I took the biscuit and gave it to Duncan, who wolfed it down.

"You have a nice day, ma'am," the man said. "You, too, Duncan." The truck whined as he put it in gear, then it rumbled down the road.

Grinning till my face hurt, I leaned over and ruffled Duncan's hair. "Duncan. We are so *home.*"

THIRTY-EIGHT

....

"Where did you get this?" Mary walked around the shiny maroon truck.

"Rented it." I turned on the truck and the engine roared.

My brother-in-law Jack had offered me my late father's bedroom furniture. Shipping it from Denver would be too costly and Flora, my old Dodge Ram, couldn't be expected to make a six-hundred-mile trip.

A local car rental agency ran weekend specials that started on Friday afternoon and ended on Monday morning. By driving hard, Mary and I could get to Colorado on Saturday and attend a birthday party for my niece, Jacquie. Both Jacquie and her sister, Kim, had new babies I wanted to see. On Sunday, we would load the furniture and drive back, arriving home late. It would be a fast trip, but August offered good weather and dependable roads.

I turned off the truck's engine. "I'll go in the house and get Duncan."

It was a foot higher to climb into the truck than into my car. With his poor vision and painful joints, Duncan sometimes faltered when jumping into the backseat of my car. When he had to scramble to regain his balance or try again, he looked around, embarrassed, to see if anyone had seen. There was no way he could get into this truck.

I lifted him onto the floor of the backseat, then helped him onto the seat, where I'd placed a blanket to protect the pristine seat from dog hairs.

"He's giving you a dirty look," Mary said. I knew he disliked being lifted, but how could he get into this truck without help? When I petted him, he looked away.

"I brought some CDs we can both enjoy," Mary said.

I gave her a skeptical look. Maybe she thought I enjoyed dark, alternative music.

"Really," she insisted.

"The Beatles?" I asked.

"I said that we could both enjoy."

"Who then?"

"Johnny Cash." She slipped a disk into the machine.

"What makes you think I like Johnny Cash?"

"Because he's old."

I hadn't ever much liked Cash, but the songs were familiar, and in a
few minutes Mary and I were bouncing and singing in loud voices.
Duncan leaned over the seat to get in on the fun, and we patted his
head in rhythm.

At a rest stop, I snapped the leash on Duncan. I opened the
truck's back door, and he gazed down at the ground.

"It's too far," I said, and lifted him out. He looked up from the
place where I'd set him and gave me another scolding look. Then
he forgave me and broke into a trot, pulling me around the pet area.
He crouched and ran at me, trying to get me into a game. I ran at
him. It felt good to move after driving.

Duncan took a long drink from his bowl, then I lifted him onto
the backseat. He lost his happy look. We drove until very late before
we got a motel. It was dark, so I didn't have to see Duncan's admon-
ishing look when I lifted him from the truck.

In the morning, Mary and I went to a café for breakfast. After
breakfast, we found a place behind the restaurant where Duncan,
always a morning person, could scamper, play, and pee.

This time when I bent over to lift him to the truck, he moved
away. Before I straightened up, he slipped past me. Mustering as much
force as he could, he jumped onto the truck ledge. He only made it
with his front paws, but I grabbed his rear end and pushed him the
rest of the way. He turned and gazed at me, deeply satisfied with himself. From the truck floor, he jumped onto the backseat, where he

assumed a dignified, seated position. "I am not helpless!" his expression said.

We rolled into Denver at noon, then headed for the mountain community where my niece's birthday would be celebrated. After the party, Mary and I stopped at Red Rocks Park.

I pointed at recesses in the rock. "The famous dinosaur tracks." I took her to see the amphitheater, which she'd heard of, and gave Duncan a good exercise walk up and down the amphitheater stairs. Exercise helped his flexibility.

We had a routine for loading now. I would open the truck door. Duncan would give me a warning look, and I would stand back. He would take aim for the truck's floor. I have no idea how much or how little he could see; often, he seemed to be jumping blindly. Even so, he wanted to do it himself and didn't seem to mind if he had to repeat an attempt. He permitted me to catch his tail end and help him up, which must have seemed to him less of an indignity than being lifted.

On the other end, when we disembarked, I opened the truck door for him and he studied the ground for a long time. He jumped to the truck's floor, then jumped out. He didn't land gracefully on the pavement, but he got there on his own.

That night, walking Duncan around Jack's neighborhood, it came to me this might be Duncan's last road trip. I stopped, sat down on a grassy hill, and pulled him onto my lap. "You are wonderful company," I told him.

He put his nose to mine. For years I'd worried, excessively perhaps, about losing him, and he had simply kept going. But his limitations were increasing.

I left him in the truck overnight, padding the seat with washable mattress pads and blankets. As it happened Duncan did not have any accidents in the truck, but accidents were starting to happen more frequently. When they did, he hung his head, tucked his tail, and looked apologetic.

On Sunday, Jack, helped by Jacquie's husband, Chris, loaded the furniture into the truck. Mary and I drove across Wyoming with a headwind. I delivered Mary to our rendezvous spot, and she headed off for Utah, where she was attending college.

The first snow arrived a month later, and after that, winter set in. I took only two road trips—one with Duncan to Salt Lake City to see Mary, and another without him at Christmastime to pick up Matt, Shane, and Shane's girlfriend, Amy, at the Salt Lake airport. There wasn't room in the car for Duncan.

When we arrived at home, Amy met Duncan. She said, "Here you are! I've heard so much about you."

"You should have seen him when he was younger," Shane said. "He understood conversation, knew exactly what we were saying. He had a huge vocabulary. And he could do lots of tricks."

Duncan smiled at Shane, maybe understanding he was receiving compliments though he couldn't hear what they were.

"He's still a wonderful dog," Amy said. "You can tell how smart he is."

Mimi begged to sit on Amy's lap, which she permitted, but we restrained the exuberant Shakespeare, who outweighed Amy.

On Christmas Eve, Matt found Duncan huddled behind the stairway. Duncan's ears drooped, and he was trembling.

"Is he sick?" Matt asked.

"I wonder if he's had a stroke."

As was his habit when sick, Duncan looked humiliated. Matt sat on the floor and petted him, assuring him he didn't need to be embarrassed.

"Maybe he's decided to die when we're all home," Matt said.

I wanted Duncan to go whatever way he preferred; still, I felt heartsick.

The trembling stopped after a time, but for several hours after that, Duncan hunkered in a corner, trying to stay out of sight.

By the next morning, the illness that had looked so serious had passed. When we gathered to open presents, Duncan joined us, wagging and happy. When I went outside to do chores, Duncan ran ahead of me, biting at snow and begging me to chase him.

Matt took extra time to say good-bye to Duncan when it was time for him to leave. This had been Matt's practice for the past two or three Christmases because of the possibility he wouldn't see Duncan again. The likelihood of a final good-bye was growing.

THIRTY-NINE

I awoke to a beloved old muzzle insinuating itself onto my pillow.
Bright moonlight coming through my bedroom window allowed me
to see Duncan's filmy eyes and the gray hairs on his nose.

"Morning, Duncan." I had gone to bed mournful and slept fitfully.
Now awakening, I felt instant sorrow.

"We can change our minds," I said. Of course I could. I could
call the vet and say, "Cancel my 10 A.M. appointment for Duncan."

"Let's see how the morning goes," I told him.

I took Duncan downstairs, let him out into the chilly night, and
put on the teapot. It was only 4 A.M., but I wouldn't be going back to
bed. Ronna had set aside her morning to go with me to the vet, but if
I changed my mind, she would support that, too.

The night before I'd removed the tarps and rocks covering a large
hole that Don, my writer friend, had dug in the back field the previous fall. "If Duncan were to die during the winter, you couldn't dig
a grave in frozen ground. And I know you want him buried here,"
he'd said.

No dirt had caved in on the hole. I'd expected mice would have
overtaken it, but only one scurried up the dirt wall and disappeared
into the weeds.

Mary and I soon would be driving to Texas for Shane's graduation from law school, and in late May it would be too hot to keep
Duncan in the car for long. Leaving him in a motel during graduation activities wouldn't work, either, because Duncan's control over
his functions had weakened so much.

Boarding him at a kennel offered another option, but Duncan's hold on life seemed so fragile, I was terrified he might die in my absence. I couldn't stand the thought of my loyal dog being alone at the end of his life.

Shane's graduation forced an issue that had to be decided. Duncan's loss of bowel control was causing him considerable distress. Even when I took him on a short car trip to town, he was apt to have an accident. I kept a sheet on the backseat and I would say, "Don't worry about it, buddy," but Duncan would suck his tail against his stomach and look miserable. In the house after a mess, he would slink to the door and hang his head. I was working at home, but even so, I couldn't take him out often enough to avoid messes.

Duncan appeared on the porch and I let him in. I started mixing a batch of pancakes. My best buttermilk recipe, the one Duncan used to walk on his hind legs for. Duncan watched me pour pancakes on the griddle, or, if he couldn't see them, he knew they were there by the smell.

"As many as you want." No more worries about keeping Duncan slim and fit.

He ate seven, wolfing them down appreciatively. *He still has quality of life. Maybe I won't do it.* The sun peeked over the eastern hills. I couldn't help feeling hopeful I could avoid the trip to the vet.

Matt had suggested on the phone that Duncan might like a final chance to play in a sprinkler. "Just a lawn sprinkler," Matt said.

The night before, I'd turned on a sprinkler, but Duncan had shown no interest. It was morning now, Duncan's favorite time, so I was willing to try again.

"Come on, Dunc." I moved the sprinkler to the driveway to improve its visibility. I took him near it so he could feel the spray. He sat down near it, blinked as droplets fell on his head, and gazed into the distance.

The previous night, I'd also tried to interest him in a last game of Frisbee. It had been years since he'd been able to jump and catch one, but I thought I might be able to roll one on the grass for him.

He'd shown no interest in it, either. Maybe he couldn't see it, despite that I'd tossed it under his nose.

A walk with all the dogs—surely Duncan would enjoy that. The morning was bright with no wind, and beginning to warm. I got Mimi from her pen and put Shakespeare on a leash.

Mimi dashed around me in circles, excited as usual. She tried to get Duncan to race with her. Duncan trotted toward the back field, following Mimi. Shakespeare bolted forward; I pulled on the leash, trying to get control of him.

Warm spring days had made the hay higher than my ankles. I pulled Shakespeare to a halt and looked around for the other two dogs. Mimi was tearing through the field and had almost reached the sagebrush hill. No sign of Duncan. I looked back toward the house and saw him sitting at the edge of the hayfield, detached and tired.

I probably ought to take him in.

Ronna came at 9:30. She gave me an inquisitive look.

"I think so," I said. "I wish I were certain."

Ronna got in the passenger seat, and I helped Duncan into the backseat. We'd barely started out the driveway when I smelled something. I turned around. Duncan had pooped. He looked miserable.

"It's okay," I told him. I told Ronna, "He just went ten minutes ago."

"Maybe he's giving you the go-ahead."

We arrived at the vet clinic. Ronna and I traded a look, and I helped Duncan out of the back.

Inside, the receptionist asked, "Do you plan to stay with him?"

"Yes."

"Taking him home with you?"

"Yes."

"Let's have you fill out the paperwork." The receptionist gave me her kindest smile.

Tears started down my face and the pen shook in my hand.

An old man came out from an examining room carrying a cat in a carrier. He stopped to pet Duncan. "What a pretty dog this is. He's a kind dog, too, I can tell that."

Duncan gave the man's fingers a polite lick.

"Hey, feller, I think you like me."

It was so like Duncan, making people feel special until the end.

"I'll just put you back here in this room," the receptionist said, "and the vet will be here in a minute."

Duncan sat down between Ronna and me. He extended his head for petting, first to Ronna, then to me.

"Good Duncan," Ronna said.

"Good, good dog," I said.

The veterinarian wasn't someone I knew. I felt a little disappointed we didn't have Rhonda, the clinic's owner, who had treated Duncan through the years, though, for all that, he had enjoyed radiant health and been to the vet infrequently.

The doctor introduced herself and asked me to put Duncan on the table.

I lifted him up. He was lighter than he'd been a year ago.

"How old?"

"Sixteen."

If the doctor said, in her professional judgment, "He could live another year or two," I'd remove him from the table and take him home, and make arrangements to board him while we were in Texas.

"He had a long life," she said. She wrapped a piece of tubing around his paw and tied it.

"The way this works, it's an overdose of anesthetic and—"

"I've been through it before."

"I might have trouble finding a vein on him. On these older dogs—"

Suddenly she jumped and exclaimed, "Oh!"

"What happened?" I asked.

"He snapped."

I was incredulous. Not Duncan.

I couldn't suppress a smile. " 'Do not go gentle into that good night. . . .' " I said, quoting Dylan Thomas.

" 'Old age should burn and rave at close of day,' " Ronna continued.

" 'Rage, rage against the dying of the light,' " I recited, feeling momentary happiness. Duncan, dependably sweet into old age, knew how to snap. And he understood this was the appropriate time to do it.

"I'll go get a muzzle," the vet said.

"Duncan." I petted his head. "There's fire in the old dog."

The doctor returned and placed a soft cotton muzzle over his nose. It looked so out of place on Duncan I felt sad all over again. Still, I couldn't quite shake feeling proud of him.

"Hold him around the body tightly," she said.

"Gladly."

The vet put the medicine into his vein. Duncan sighed. I felt him slump.

The vet checked his heart with her stethoscope and nodded. "I'll just leave you alone here. Take as long as you want."

She closed the door. I put my head in my hands and started to sob. Ronna patted my shoulder, but she was crying, too. Duncan had been a perennial companion on our walks.

"This is really hard," I choked.

I carried Duncan's body to the car.

"Are you all right to drive?" Ronna asked.

"No." I handed her the keys.

At home, Ronna helped me carry Duncan to the grave. We laid him gently in the hole and covered him with a blanket. I placed the new Frisbee beside him, and an old ball. Then I shoveled dirt over him.

"Want to go for a walk?" Ronna asked.

"Yes."

The day had warmed to a mild spring temperature. We walked to the stop sign at the end of the mile, and then returned.

As we approached the house Ronna asked, "Is Mimi out?"

"No. She never gets out of the pen."

"I just saw a Border collie pass between our two cars."

We were silent.

After awhile I asked, "Was it Duncan?"

Ronna said, "Is he letting you know he's okay?"

She stayed and had a cup of tea with me. She asked, "Why do you dog lovers do it? It looks so hard."

"I'll have to get back to you on that one."

She got ready to leave. "Are you sure you're all right?"

"Yeah. I want to write an e-mail to the kids." I thanked her and hugged her good-bye.

I was at the computer when my longtime friend Ray called. "How did it go? Are you awfully sad?"

"Awfully sad," I said. I was standing by the upstairs phone, gazing out the front window. Then I saw, apparently in the backyard, but reflected in the front window glass, a dog of indeterminate color creeping past in a Border collie sneak.

"Just a minute," I told Ray. I ran downstairs and looked out the back window. The backyard was empty. I ran to the front window. No dog there, either.

I came back to the phone and told Ray, "That was odd. I thought I saw a dog. It seemed like it might be in the backyard, but reflected in the front window. But I checked, and there's no dog in either place."

"What did it look like?"

"Indistinct. I couldn't make it out. That's why I thought it was a reflection."

"About Duncan's size."

"Yeah."

"That's how they come back from the other side," Ray said matter-of-factly. "Reflected in glass or mirrors."

I didn't know whether I bought that, but it made me smile. I liked the idea of Duncan paying me a visit.

As I was going to sleep that night, I wished for Duncan to come to me in a dream. That had happened to me once when I'd lost a cat, and had happened to others I knew who'd lost animals. But Duncan didn't come in a dream that night, or that week, or anytime after.

Ray said that was because he'd already returned to say he was all right.

FORTY

....

I called Ronna the next day and said, "I can answer your question now."

In the silence on the other end, I heard Ronna trying to puzzle out what I was talking about.

"How did you sleep?" she asked.

"Rough. But I'm beginning to find some peace. I've thought about your question about why we dog lovers keep getting attached, even though we know we'll watch the dog grow old and die."

"So, tell me," she said.

"You've heard some of this before, but I'm going to say it anyway because it has traction for me right now.

"You've heard plenty of times how dogs love us unconditionally. They love us when we're cross and neglectful, sick or sorrowing. Who else does that unfailingly, except God? Only God sometimes seems remote, unlike the dog at our side.

"And dogs show us how to live big. They do everything with gusto, whether it's drinking from the toilet or heading down the driveway for a walk they've taken a thousand times before. Every day is new, every activity is the best. In their company, we're lifted out of our human concerns and remember what it's like to be excited.

"But here's what strikes me as most important. And it's not about what they give us, but about something we give ourselves. We get to love a dog full out."

"Okay."

"Our days on this earth are short, even if we live to a fine old age. Something we want out of this brief life is to love grandly. But we don't often give our hearts without reserve. With dogs, though, we can. Our feeling isn't complicated by hurts of the past or worries about our independence. We feel no need to be coy or cautious. The humans we love have aspirations that don't always mesh with ours, and when we come up against those different longings, we rein ourselves in. But we aren't so scared about loving a dog.

"We loved our babies recklessly. Yet, even as we gazed at them in their cribs, struck dumb by the immensity of our feelings, we glimpsed the day when they would walk out the door, tall and independent. Something whispered to us that we must hedge our love a bit, because those magnificent babies didn't belong to us.

"But a dog doesn't wish to go out and have a life of his own; he only wants to share life with his person."

"But you'll lose the dog."

"Dogs live in such a way that we forget their mortality. We can't imagine the day when the dog's exuberant spirit will be extinguished. So we open our hearts to them and discover our hearts hold an extravagant amount of love. We let it flow out. Think what this does for us as people. Think how that enlarges us."

"And makes it worth it?"

"Yes! Loving full out gives us a way to defy death. Death surrounds us, but love holds its own against loss."

There was no response for a minute. Then Ronna said, "I think this means you'll go on loving dogs."

It was hell getting used to being without Duncan.

I was ready to leave for Shane's graduation from law school. I'd loaded the car with tent, sleeping bag, and suitcase. All I needed to do was return to the house for Duncan.

Then I remembered.

It went like that all day.

There's the Malad rest area, Duncan. I'll pull over and you can pee. Remember the time we walked the upper path and ran into a couple on a bench who were getting it on? You wanted to stop, but I tugged you past them.

In Salt Lake City, I stopped and picked up Mary. I wanted to take a back country route through small, picturesque towns, so we studied our maps and decided on an itinerary. One road we knew from before. I'd driven it when delivering or picking up Mary when she'd been part of the wilderness program, first as a student, then as an instructor.

"Remember that convenience store, Mom? We didn't get there until two in the morning and you were so sleepy? We were surprised the store was still open."

"There's a stream behind it where Duncan got a drink."

He had traveled with me so much, it felt strange not to have his needs to consider. Someone might have suggested I'd gained care-freeness now that I didn't have to care for an old dog. But I had no such feeling at all. Duncan had remained good company even in infirmity.

We took our time, stopped to take pictures, and sought out grocery stores and restaurants where Mary, a vegetarian, could find something to eat. The first night in our tent, the wind came up and nearly blew us away. The next night, we found a motel.

We pulled into Austin at midday. Shane's girlfriend, Amy, who worked for a bed-and-breakfast Internet business, had found a beautiful B and B for us in Austin. Jack, my brother-in-law, and nieces, Jacquie and Kim, were scheduled to arrive later in the day.

I'd cried plenty before and after Duncan's death, but I shed no tears during the trip—until the graduation ceremony, when graduates were each given a minute to say something. Most used the time to thank those who'd supported them during the tough law school years. When it was Shane's turn, he thanked family members; his girlfriend, Amy; "and Duncan." My eyes sprang tears.

I thought tender sentiment for an animal might be unique to Shane, but two other graduates acknowledged animal helpers. A young man recognized Ralph, a dog who always gave him encouragement, and a young woman appreciated Rosie, the cat "who sat on my open textbooks." It didn't seem a stretch that animals would be thanked for helping their people attain large accomplishments. Who could assess how much it meant to be the recipient of devotion from a four-footed friend?

The next October, Lala, the only survivor from the Gang of Four, which had included Duncan, Gracie, and Aurora, died. Lala had been acting clingy and wanting to be held a lot, and once again had been losing weight. I found her dead on the porch one day. I buried her beside the barn near Aurora, whom she'd never liked much.

An era had ended. Except for Rainbow, the animals Matt and Shane had grown up with had all died. Mimi, whom Mary had gotten for her fourteenth birthday, was beginning to get gray hairs on her muzzle.

New animals would come to each of us, and with them, new chapters. But the years when we'd warmed newborn lambs in the kitchen, attended fairs and sheep shows, and hosted 4-H meetings in the basement had been important ones, and we'd had extraordinary animals to share them with.

I considered myself fortunate to have known a number of dogs, cats, sheep, horses, cattle, goats, hogs, llamas, a canary, and a turtle. But Duncan had staked the greatest claim on my heart. He'd come into my life as a dignified puppy and had grown into a complex mix of earnestness and unrestrained joy. He'd been more than an animal friend; he'd been a valuable teacher.

Duncan had possessed considerable intelligence, but he also took time to be observant. On those few occasions when he miscalculated how to behave, he was willing to change tactics. In the past, I often had persisted with behaviors even when they netted poor results. I hoped I could remember Duncan's better approach.

After Duncan died, I learned the Celtic origin of his name. Dark-haired warrior. That would fit only if you believed warrior described someone who stayed strong in spirit no matter what.

Reviewing the years and recalling the roads I'd passed over, I could acknowledge the struggles. But I also gave the joyful moments their due and appreciated the fine animal companion who'd trotted beside me, generously sharing his happiness and sharing in mine.

For those of us who have been loved by a great dog, who have, in turn, loved the dog back, we can say, and this is not too large a statement, we have known Glory in our lives.

Spring

FORTY-ONE

She angled toward me on impossibly long willow-branch legs, and watched me with great brown eyes. Her foal ears pitched forward like leaning tepees. Translucent, pearly skin stretched over her bony ribs and her belly made a sucked-up arch. That was okay. Almost any day-old foal was gangly. This foal showed hints of future good muscling in her shoulders and rump.

She kept her eye on me but continued to come forward. When she got within touching distance, I eased my hand toward her. Softly, I ran my fingertips down her white neck. She felt like warm silk. Instead of moving away, the foal moved closer. She snugged against my waist. I reached my arm over her and began stroking her side. I imagined her newborn spirit warming the pads of my fingers.

Honey, my new Appaloosa mare, paid us little heed. This was her second colt and maybe she saw no reason to fuss over it. Or maybe Honey's generally easygoing nature made her more interested in tender grasses emerging in the corral than keeping a close eye on her foal.

As the foal leaned against me, I kept still as a tree. "I think we're going to be good friends." She didn't look up when I spoke but continued to stare at my denim-clad hip.

"Are you cold?" It had been a cool spring, and though the sun was shining, I wondered if it might feel a bit chilly to a newborn. Was she snuggled against me for warmth?

I stroked her chest and belly to see if she felt cold. She didn't.

"I guess you're just friendly."

Her tepee ears flickered.

She was fragile like a hand-carved figurine. Only no human could have created anything so perfect.

I'd already decided that if Honey gave birth to a filly, I would name her Maiah, after the guardian spirit of farms.

"Maiah," I said aloud.

Her round eyes lifted, and she looked at my face.

"I love you, Maiah."

Love at first meeting. Bonding of the instantaneous kind.

"Here I go again," I said.

ACKNOWLEDGMENTS

I thank these people who helped with the manuscript:

Ronna Marwil, for jumbo encouragement and spot-on advice,

Debbie Empey, for her expertise on Border collies,

Debbie Empey, Dave Clark, and Jamie Jonas, members of my writers' group,

Tina Welling, for impressive feedback and jokes in the margin,

My editor, Karyn Marcus, for asking penetrating questions and being an effective cheerleader,

My agent, Jennifer Cayea, for a steadily cheerful outlook and helpful suggestions,

My neighbor Linda Demmer, who helped me recall details of the neighborhood circus.